The Genesis
of Methodism

The Genesis of Methodism

Frederick Dreyer

Lehigh
University
Press

Bethlehem: Lehigh University Press
London: Associated University Presses

Associated University Presses
440 Forsgate Drive
Cranbury, NJ 08512

Associated University Presses
16 Barter Street
London WC1A 2AH, England

Associated University Presses
P.O. Box 338, Port Credit
Mississauga, Ontario
Canada L5G 4L8

The paper used in this publication meets the requirements
of the American National Standard for Permanence of Paper
for Printed Library Materials Z39.48-1984.

Library of Congress Cataloging-in-Publication Data

Dreyer, Frederick A., 1932–
    The genesis of Methodism / Frederick Dreyer.
        p.   cm.
    Includes bibliographical references and index.
    ISBN 0-934223-56-4 (alk. paper)
    1. Methodism—History—18th century.   2. Wesley, John, 1703–1791.
I. Title.
BX8231.D74   1999
287'.09'033—dc21   99-13975
                                                                            CIP

PRINTED IN THE UNITED STATES OF AMERICA

To
Betty

Toutes les origines sont obscures, les origines religieuses encore plus que les autres. Produits des instincts spontanés de la nature humaine, les religions ne se rappellent pas plus leur enfance que l'adulte ne se rappelle l'histoire de son premier âge et les phases successives du développement de sa conscience: chrysalides mystérieuses, elles n'apparaissent au grand jour que dans la parfaite maturité de leur formes.

Renan, "Mahomet et les origines de l'islamisme"

Contents

Acknowledgments

THIS IS A SHORT BOOK, BUT NOT ONE THAT WAS WRITTEN QUICKLY. iT IS MY GOOD fortune to teach in a history department that is realistic in its expectations and where it is recognized that scholarship takes time. Canadians, as a rule, do not like the eighteenth century. As subjects of the King of France, we were defeated in the Seven Years War; and in the American Revolution, as subjects of the King of England. Happily, the University of Western Ontario is a place where interest in the century thrives and an audience can always be found to hear someone who wants to talk about it. This is due to the efforts of Roger Emerson, who tirelessly presides over our eighteenth-century society and makes sure that we all get a proper hearing. I owe much to the encouragement of Ian Steele and Neville Thompson. I am also indebted to the staff of Weldon Library, particularly to David Newman and John Hoover who made it possible to purchase the Beyreuther and Meyer edition of the Zinzendorf *Schriften*. Without this, I might have written a book on the origins of Methodism, but not the same sort of book with the same sort of argument. I am especially indebted to the staff of the Interlibrary Loan Office for their help in getting works that Weldon does not own. Linda Sabathy-Judd has been unstinting in her efforts to correct my deficiencies in reading and speaking German. Douglas Adams and John Schuit have taught me much about evangelical divinity, to the first I owe a better understanding of salvation by faith, and to the second, of conviction of sin. Chapter 4 draws heavily on two essays I have published elsewhere: "Faith and Experience in the Thought of John Wesley," *American Historical Review,* vol. 88, no. 1 (February 1983): 12–30, and "A 'Religious Society under Heaven': John Wesley and the Identity of Methodism," *Journal of British Studies,* vol. 25, no. 1 (January 1986): 62–83, by the North American Conference on British Studies. All rights reserved. I thank the American Historical Association for permission to reprint the first essay and the University of Chicago Press, to reprint the second. Debts are owed to many people. My wife has been a constant support and to her this book is dedicated.

9

The Genesis
of Methodism

1

Schism

In history, it is often hard to say when things get started. Methodism counts as a happy exception, for a commencement can be claimed that is precise to the very day: Wednesday, 23 July 1740. On that day, John Wesley and a small group of friends assembled in the London suburb of Moorfields on the premises of an old, disused iron works known as the Foundery. Wesley had acquired the lease and after the meeting of the 23rd the Foundery was to serve as the headquarters of the Methodist revival. Three days before the meeting, Wesley and his friends had seceded from a devotional society that met in Fetter Lane. What distinguished the Foundery from Fetter Lane was the latter's connection with the United Brethren in Germany. The Brethren, in English usage, are better known as the Moravians. In 1738, Fetter Lane had been set up under the direction of Peter Böhler, a missionary who belonged to the United Brethren and who was passing through London on his way to the American colonies. In 1740, membership of the Fetter Lane was being guided by a second missionary, Philip Molther. Wesley seceded from Fetter Lane in protest against Molther's leadership. No formal tie linked Fetter Lane with the Brethren. But in its purpose and constitution, it resembled societies that the Brethren had founded elsewhere. Fetter Lane would reform itself in 1742 as a society and assume an identity that was explicitly Moravian.[1]

What provoked the schism was a dispute over who possessed saving faith and who was entitled to receive holy communion as a member of the society. In Brethren societies in Germany, members attended the local church together to receive the sacraments.[2] This practice was followed at Fetter Lane. In Germany, of course, the local church would be Lutheran or Reformed; in London, it was Anglican. We know that, on at least two occasions, the Fetter Lane society attended St. Paul's for joint communion. Wesley's brother, Charles,

13

who also belonged to the society, administered communion to members in private houses.[3] *Das Sprechen,* or conversation, was another institution in communion discipline. Four or five brethren met under the direction of a leader appointed by the society. There they examined each other and decided on their fitness for receiving the sacrament. A fault of temperament and behavior or a lapse in faith could result in a member being excluded from the service. Because the appointed service was usually conducted by a minister not connected with the society, it is perhaps more accurate to speak of the member's exclusion at the service from the company of his brethren. Who administered the rite was unimportant; who received it was not.[4]

How far the Fetter Lane society had gone in its process of Moravianization is hard to say. The record makes no explicit reference to *das Sprechen.* Yet, common attendance at communion was established from the start. Also established from the start were the small groups or bands in which members might talk about their spiritual state. In the band, the member was required to speak "as freely, plainly and concisely as he can, the real state of his heart, with his several temptations and deliverances." This injunction is printed in the general rules adopted on Peter Böhler's advice, 1 May 1738. In Wesley's collected works we find a set of rules that relate specifically to the bands. These rules are dated 25 December 1738. If anything, the inquisitorial or confessional function of the band is reinforced here. The member must speak to the state of his own soul. After that, he should address the other members and ask them in order "as many and as searching questions as may be, concerning their state, sins, and temptations." New members might be asked whether they had experienced "the forgiveness of sins" and enjoy "peace with God through our Lord Jesus Christ." "Have you the witness of God's Spirit with your spirit, that you are a child of God?" At every meeting of the band, each member was to be asked: "What known sins have you committed since our last meeting?" "What temptations have you met with?" "How were you delivered?" "What have you thought, said or done, of which you doubt whether it be sin or not?"[5]

It is likely some form of pre-communion examination and selection was set up in Fetter Lane at the outset. Certainly, who should receive communion, and who should not, was the issue that precipitated the schism. In October 1739, Philip Molther had turned up in London as the representative of the Moravians. From Molther's perspective, the members had misunderstood what it was to be converted and had embarked on a vain effort to justify themselves by their own efforts. "The good people," he said,

> not knowing rightly what they wanted, had adopted many most extraordinary usages. The very first time I entered their meeting, I was alarmed and almost terror-stricken at hearing their sighing and groaning, their whining and howling, which strange proceeding they called the demonstration of the Spirit and power.

The members aspired to faith and did not know how to attain it. Molther commenced with the instructions in the bands. "From morning till night," a member wrote, "he is engaged in conversing with souls and laboring to bring them into better order; they get a great confidence towards him. . . . The false foundation many had made has been discovered, and now speedily will be laid in many souls the only foundation, Christ Jesus."[6] The mistake of the members lay in thinking that the way to faith was, first, through consciousness of their own guilt. This was standard German Pietism and something the Brethren had once believed themselves. In 1740, consciousness of guilt was out; in its place, the Moravians encouraged their adherents to focus attention on the so-called "blood and wounds." This meant that faith commenced with an awareness of Christ's death on the cross. "Blood and wounds" was the right foundation; consciousness of sin was the wrong one. Band members who could not grasp this probably were discouraged from taking communion. It was the communion issue that confronted Wesley, who had been absent from London on Molther's arrival:

> In the evening I met the women of our society at Fetter Lane, where some of our brethren strongly intimated that none of them had any true faith, and then asserted, in plain terms: (1) that, till they had true faith, they ought to be "still"; that is . . . to abstain from the means of grace . . .— the Lord's Supper in particular; (2) that the ordinances are not means of grace, there being no other means than Christ.[7]

It was hard to quarrel over these matters and not raise questions of theology. Because the society did not agree in its conception of saving faith, it could not agree on its communion list. Yet, what forced the dispute was not insistence on credal orthodoxy. On neither side was credal orthodoxy thought to be important for salvation. But this was not an issue where people could agree to differ. Formed to encourage brotherhood and common worship, the society could not decide who was eligible for worship and who was not. The problem was practical, and schism could not be avoided. Wesley had bought the Foundery eight months before he finally seceded from Fetter Lane. The lease cost £115, repairs and improvements another £480. For this, he had gone into debt.[8] Possibly, separation was something Wesley had intended from the beginning. In April, Charles Wesley thought of it as inevitable. Still, further efforts were made to reach a compromise. On 11 June, the membership of the bands was reconstituted. Those who agreed with John Wesley were reassigned to separate bands, to meet under his direction.[9] Two days later, he assembled his people for common worship. "A great part of our society joined with us in prayer, and kept, I trust an acceptable fast unto the Lord." This was schism in practice, if not in principle. But Wesley still thought of himself as a member of the Fetter Lane society, and in his journal still refers to it as our "own Society." Also, in his journal, he records further meetings with the Brethren where efforts were made to reach a settlement. Wednesday, July 9: "I came to an explanation once more with them all together; but with no effect at all." Tuesday, July 15: "We had yet another conference at large, but in vain; for all continued in their own opinions." On the 16th another meeting was held. "We continued in useless debate till about eleven. I then gave them up to God." Two days later, Wesley's party met and resolved to leave. "We all saw the thing was now come to a crisis, and were therefore unanimously agreed what to do." On 20 July, Wesley went to Fetter Lane for the last time. It was a Sunday, ironically a date set aside for the celebration of a love feast. This was a simple meal in which the members ate together and celebrated their Christian brotherhood. Wesley attended and presumably took part in the love feast. When it came to an end, he made a short statement of the differences that divided him and the Brethren. No reconciliation was possible, he said. "I have borne with you long, hoping you would turn. But as I find you more and more confirmed in the error of your ways, nothing now remains but that I should give you up to God." Turning to his friends, he concluded: "You that are of the same judgment, follow me." Eighteen or nineteen left with him. Three days later, they assembled at the Foundery for their first meeting as an independent society.[10]

John Wesley was an ordained minister in the Church of England and a fellow of Lincoln College, Oxford. For two years he had served as incumbent in a missionary parish in Savannah, Georgia. His father and two brothers were also ministers. Wesley never ceased to be a member of the Church of England and one of its ministers. Many of the early Methodists may also have belonged to the church. It was a preoccupation of his leadership lest Methodism turn itself into another version of English nonconformity. All this is true, yet it is important to recognize that Methodism was never intended to work within the structure of the established church. Wesley was not the parson in Moorfields; the society he formed was not a vestry society set up with the approval of the incumbent. Such societies existed, and Wesley knew about them; had he so chosen, it is possible Methodism could have developed as a network of parish societies whose members were recruited from the parish congregation and whose leaders were provided by the parish ministry. This did not happen. In Moorfields, Wesley was a private person, and the existence of the society owed nothing to his status as a clergyman. When Methodism spread beyond Moorfields and new societies were set up elsewhere, it was done in defiance of parish boundaries. This had, in principle, been decided on even before Wesley had made his break with the Brethren. "I look upon all the world as my parish; thus far I mean, that in whatever part of it I am I judge it meet, right, and my bounden duty to declare, unto all that are willing to hear, the glad tidings of salvation."[11]

One of the mistakes that is often made in understanding the Methodist Revival is to think of it as a lost opportunity for the church, where, with more responsiveness and imagination, Wesley's energy and genius might have been harnessed in the service of church expansion. This is not what Wesley intended; the Society was not to be annexed by the vestry. Wesley's plans, moreover, never included a settlement with the Church of England, whereby his movement might be regularized. Certainly, there were Methodists who sought such a settlement. In 1775, for instance, a plan was put forward to have Methodist preachers ordained by Anglican bishops, but nothing came of it.[12] Even supposing that ordination is something the bishops would have given, we cannot assume it was something Wesley sought. Methodism had to work outside the parish system. If his preachers ceased to be itinerants moving from parish to parish, "be their talents ever so great, they will ere long grow dead themselves, and so will most of those that hear them." The ideal of one parson to each parish was denied: "Nor can I believe it was ever the will of our Lord that any congregation should have one teacher only. We have found by long and constant experience that a frequent change of teachers is best."[13] Wesley's opposition had nothing to do with the fact that most parish ministers were anti-evangelical. He refused to yield to parish discipline even in cases where the minister was virtually a Methodist and preached evangelical conversion. If the minister wanted to help out, it had to be done on Methodist terms. As long as he observed the proprieties of parish discipline and insisted on his status as parish minister, his assistance was discouraged. Such parsons saved no one, Wesley argued. "No, not one, till they were *irregular* . . . formed irregular Societies and took in laymen to assist them. Can there be a stronger proof that God is pleased with irregular even more than with regular preaching?"[14] The preference for *irregularity* exacerbated his quarrel with the evangelical clergy. Every man's parish belonged to Wesley's world. No parson, however godly and diligent, could be sure an irregular ministry would not be started on his own doorstep. Methodism was not meant to work as a branch of the Church of England.[15]

The second pattern of development Methodism resisted was the one set by English Dissent. The schism had occurred within the society at Fetter Lane, not within the Church of England. Nothing had happened at Fetter Lane that affected Wesley's status as a member of the Church of England. Methodists were not Dissenters. Membership in the Methodist society entailed no separation from the church. Wesley's pronouncements on the point were frequent and emphatic: "Whoever leaves the Church will leave the Methodists"; "If ever the Methodists in general were to leave the Church, I must leave them"; "I am a Church-of-England man; and . . . in the Church I will live and die, unless I am thrust out"; "I will not leave the Church of England as by law established while the breath of God is in my nostrils."[16] At the conference of 1752, the Methodist preachers pledged to remain within the Church of England: "Our present call is chiefly to the members of that Church wherein we have been brought up." The pledge was reaffirmed at later conferences.[17] Methodists were not to hold their meetings at the time of church service. The proper place for a Methodist to be at that time was in the parish church. "Let all the servants in our preaching houses go to church on Sunday morning at least," the conference ordered. "Let every preacher likewise go always on Sunday morning; and when he can in the afternoon. God will bless those who go on weekdays too, as often as they have opportunity." Methodist preachers were not to assume functions that properly belonged to ordained clergy. Those who baptized were dismissed. "Whoever among us undertakes to baptise a child," wrote Wesley, "is *ipso facto* excluded from our Connexion."[18] Methodism did not claim to be a church. Any practice or usage that implied ecclesiastical status was discountenanced. Wesley warned Methodists not to call the society a "church," nor its preachers "ministers." Nor was the place where they met to be called a "meeting house." That was a term dissenters used. "Call them plain preaching-houses or chapels," he said. Methodists in Scotland were warned against borrowing church practices from the Presbyterians. "'Sessions!' 'elders!' We Methodists have no such customs." To a preacher who had convened a Methodist session in Glasgow, Wesley sent a prohibition: "I require *you* . . . immediately to disband that session (so called). . . . Discharge them from meeting any more. And if they will leave the society, let them leave it. . . . You ought to have kept to the Methodist plan from the first."[19] It was a point of pride among Methodists that they were not Dissenters—indeed, that they did not even constitute a church, attempting to do the same thing as other churches.

In time, of course, Wesley did ordain preachers to administer the sacraments; but that was ordination for export. A Methodist preacher who was priested for Scotland was *un*priested upon his return to England. North of the Tweed, Wesley addressed a preacher as *Reverend*, south of it as plain *Mr.*[20] At Wesley's death, ordinations were suspended, not to be resumed until the 1830s. Methodists did, in the end, separate from the Church of England, but that was separation by inertia. It came imperceptibly and by degrees, and no one can tell which point was critical and which was not. Until the very end of the nineteenth century, membership tickets were issued in the name of the Wesleyan Methodist *Society*, and not the Methodist *Church*.[21]

The challenge Methodism delivered to the Church of England was not made on an issue of government or doctrine. The year 1740 is not a date that bears comparison with 1662, when Anglicans and Dissenters separated from each other. In its intention and consequences, Methodism's founding in 1740 cannot be understood as an episode in the history of English Dissent.

Church and Dissent each offered a pattern of development that Methodism rejected. By an inversion of logic, however, a Methodism that cannot be explained as either Church or Dissent has come to be understood as deriving from both. Whatever contradicts Wesley's churchmanship affirms the nonconformity; whatever contradicts the nonconformity affirms the churchmanship. Thus, Methodism figures in history as a combination of irreconcilable influences. This conception, like many other aspects of Methodist scholarship, goes back to the work of the French historian, Elie Halévy. For Halévy, Methodism is the "High Church of Nonconformity," a "Nonconformist sect established by Anglican clergymen who wished to remain faithful to the Church of England." Its theology comes partly from a Puritan emphasis on justification by faith and partly from an anti-Puritan emphasis on free will and works. "This eclecticism, which logic may call inadmissible, gave novelty and force to the Puritanism revived by Wesley." The contradiction manifests itself in Methodist ecclesiology. There, says Halévy, "we find the same eclecticism, the same conciliation of contrary principles." On nonconformist considerations, Wesley encourages the layman to preach; on High Church considerations, he forbids him to administer the sacraments. "In Wesleyan organization, the hierarchical and the egalitarian principles were combined in equal portions." The two-nature theory of Methodism was first stated by Halévy in an article published in the *Revue de Paris* in 1906. It was restated—this time, to a much larger readership—in *England in 1815.* Here, Methodism is set on the "frontier of the Church of England," but its future lay in its affiliation with the Dissenters. "Thus the old establishment and the existing Free churches constituted the double environment in which the new spirit was developed. And it is only when we are acquainted with this environment that we can understand the character and estimate the importance of the Methodist revival." Methodism occupied a position "intermediate between the Establishment and the older Nonconformist bodies. It . . . constituted a transition between the former and the latter."[22] What commanded attention in Halévy's work was not how Methodism was identified but the function assigned to it in the evolution of English history. In the celebrated thesis that sparked interest and controversy, Halévy's Methodism is the Methodism thought to have stopped a revolution on the French pattern from breaking out in England. Interest and controversy were not sparked by the thesis that defined Methodism in terms of its two opposite natures. This was a novelty in fact. Nothing like it was to be found in such standard works as Leslie Stephen's *History of English Thought in the Eigh-*

teenth Century (1876) or William Lecky's *History of England in the XVIII Century* (1897). Novelty or not, however, Halévy's definition triumphed by stealth and has come to be accepted as more or less self-evident truth.

In the *Making of the English Working Class,* E. P. Thompson condemns the *ambivalence* of Methodism: "From the outset the Wesleyans fell ambiguously between Dissent and the Establishment, and did their utmost to make the worst of both worlds." What is eclecticism in Halévy emerges as "promiscuous opportunism" in Thompson. "In his theology, Wesley appears to have dispensed with the best and selected unhesitatingly the worst elements of Puritanism; if in class terms Methodism was hermaphroditic, in doctrinal terms it was a mule."[23] With less heat and perhaps more light, the two-nature theory is endorsed by Bernard Semmel in his *Methodist Revolution.* In this version, Halévy's "church and dissent" are translated into Ernst Troeltsch's "church and sect." But the change in terminology makes little difference to the point at issue. Semmel's Wesley is a "Laudian enthusiast." Like a dissenter, he is evangelical and, like Archbishop Laud, an authoritarian. His movement figures both as church and sect. "Methodism began . . . as a sect within a Church . . . but . . . it was to become . . . virtually a second National Church." Halévy's Methodism held a position *intermediate* between church and dissent. Semmel's Methodism stands "midway between sect and church, and sharing the characteristics of both." In their irregular assemblies, the Methodists resemble the Dissenters; unlike the Dissenters, their purpose was to strengthen and revitalize the church. To this double identity Semmel's Methodists owe their success. It was "a consequence of their ability to make the appeal and wield the discipline of both sect and church."[24]

As students of Methodism, Thompson and Semmel are primarily interested in its status as a revolutionary or counterrevolutionary event. Did Methodism hinder the rise of democracy in modern history? Semmel says no; Thompson says yes. Both, however, address a question first put by Halévy. It is not surprising that they should also appropriate his definition of Methodism in its ecclesiastical identity. The definition, however, is not restricted to scholars who stand in direct line of succession to Halévy. It prevails everywhere. Frank Baker tells us that, throughout his adult life, Wesley, "responded with varying degrees of enthusiasm to two fundamentally different views of the church." Baker's Wesley is half Church, half

Dissent, as is John Bowmer's. "Wesleyanism then, was neither Anglican nor Dissenting, yet it combined elements from both—a voluntary
principle with an authoritative government, a Presbyterian polity with
an Arminian theology, a gathered congregation without formal separation from the Established Church." A recent statement of two-
nature orthodoxy can be found in Michael Watts' *Dissenters*. Here,
Wesley is a combination of High Church piety and seventeenth-
century Puritanism:

> Wesley grafted on to the High Church stock from which he was reared
> the Evangelical scions of conversion and justification by faith, and for
> most of his life both original stock and the new graft grew side by side
> to the puzzlement of contemporaries and the perplexity of historians.

In Watts' opinion, it was the Dissenting half in the Methodist mixture
that was destined to prevail. Initially, the movement was Anglican,
not Dissenting. "But it was Dissent, not the Church of England, that
reaped the ultimate benefit."[25]

The two-nature definition requires us to imagine a revival whose
logic is unintelligible to its members—perhaps even to Wesley, its
leader. Either they do not know, or do not care, what it is they are
doing. The eclectic Wesley comes across as someone who, in turn,
is muddleheaded, impulsive, and, perhaps, even disingenuous. In
Thompson, he is the "promiscuous opportunist"; Methodism is used
as a device to bamboozle the working classes. In Baker, he is a
"bundle of contradictions" who achieves consistency by following
the will of God, "as he saw it from moment to moment." No plan is
consulted; Wesley improvises on the spot, receiving his inspiration
from a variety of sources. Sometimes his expedients are modeled on
the Church of England, sometimes on the sect, sometimes on nothing
at all. "Wesley was not concerned about the source, so long as the
projected method of furthering the purpose of God in Methodism
met his own peculiar brand of churchmanship—and *worked*."[26] People like this do exist. The portrayal may well prove true on empirical
grounds. On logical grounds, however, it is necessarily true as an
inference from Methodism in its two-nature definition. As long as
we think of Methodism as a combination of church and sect, we
cannot dispense with a Wesley who figures as an eclectic, an opportunist, or an improviser. Whether he deserves the reputation cannot
be decided by his own verdict. Yet it should be remembered that
eclecticism is not something Wesley ever confessed to or boasted of.

That I may say many things which have been said before, and perhaps by Calvin or Arminius, by Montanus or Barclay, or the Archbishop of Cambray, is highly probable. But it cannot thence be inferred that I hold "a medley of all their principles; —Calvinism, Arminianism, Montanism, Quakerism, Quietism, all thrown together."

Wesley insisted on the unity of his own thought. "I believe there will be found few if any real contradictions in what I have published for near thirty years." He, for one, did not think of himself as an opportunist or an eclectic.[27]

The schism at Fetter Lane did nothing to decide Wesley's status, either as a Churchman or as a Dissenter. In this respect, his status remains unchanged. It was a private society that was instituted at the Foundery, one unrelated to either church or sect. What was decided in 1740 was Wesley's status as a member of the Moravian revival. Before 1740, Wesley acted in association with the Brethren; after 1740, he did not. Whatever else it may be, Methodism can be fairly understood as a rejection of Moravianism. It is here that we find the context that makes Methodism intelligible as a historical event. What Methodism would borrow from the Church of England and what from Dissent was a question that never had to be answered before it was raised by Halévy. What would be borrowed from the Moravians, and what rejected, were questions that confronted Methodism in the very circumstances of its founding.

In their origins, the United Brethren antedate the Methodists by thirteen years. The brotherhood commenced in 1727 as a revival movement on the estates of Count Zinzendorf at Herrnhut, in Saxony. Zinzendorf's influence in the leadership of the Brethren corresponds to Wesley's influence in Methodism. Like the Methodists, the ecclesiastical identity of the Moravians is hard to pin down. In each case, the reason is the same. They began as private societies, only later and somewhat hesitantly assuming functions that are ecclesiastical. Both are better understood if thought of as private associations. The Brethren complicate matters for us by acquiring their own church, which acts as a subsection of the society. This is the Moravian church proper. As a formal institution, it began in the Hussite movement of the fifteenth century in Bohemia and Moravia. By the eighteenth century, it survived there as an underground congregation. The only place in Europe where it still functioned as a legally tolerated church with its own clergy and public service was at Lissa, in Poland, where exiles from Moravia had settled in the seventeenth century. A number of Zinzendorf's tenants were recent refugees from Moravia and had belonged to the illegal congregations deriving from the old Moravian church. These congregations had no clergy and met irregularly. It is a matter of uncertainty how much of their discipline, theology, and liturgy had survived from the fifteenth century. In Lissa, the Moravians retained the episcopal succession from the old Moravian church, but in their theology, they had become Calvinists and were closely related to Calvinist congregations in Switzerland. In Herrnhut, Moravian exiles were exposed to the influence of Lutheranism. For public service, they went to the local Lutheran church. As Brethren, they acknowledged the orthodoxy of the Augsburg Confession. Just as Wesley always insisted on his status as an Anglican, Zinzendorf insisted on his as a Lutheran. In explaining what the Brethren do, their affiliation with the old Moravian church is perhaps less important than their affiliation with Lutheran Pietism. The Moravian church was something the Society reinvented and used for its own purposes. It was the Society that ran the church, not vice versa. The Society gained possession of its church in 1735, when one of the members, David Nitschmann, was consecrated bishop. The consecration was effected through the succession that had survived in the Moravian church in Poland. In 1737, Zinzendorf had himself consecrated. It is these consecrations that give the Brethren the formal justification for ordaining their own clergy. By putting on their Moravian caps, they can do what the Methodists might have done had fortune turned one or two of their members into Anglican bishops. But, just as it is wrong to equate Methodism with the Church of England, so it is wrong to equate Zinzendorf's society with the Moravian church. The connection between the old and the reinvented Moravians stopped with the episcopal consecrations. No merger took place, and the new Moravians kept their distance from the government of the old church. At Lissa, in Poland, we find new Moravians evangelizing old Moravian congregations with the same freedom as they evangelized congregations that belonged to the Lutheran and Reformed churches. Nor did membership in the old Moravian church imply membership in the new Moravian society. An old Moravian who sought admission in Herrnhut or Herrnhaag applied on the same terms as anyone else. In this respect, the relationship between new and old Moravians is rather like the relationship between Anglicans and Methodists. Revival of the institutions of the Moravian church was not something the new Moravians had undertaken for its own sake; instead, it was forced on them by missionary work abroad. Bishops were not needed in Germany, but they were needed overseas. As soon as David Nitschmann was consecrated in 1735, he was sent to Georgia. In Europe the convert could attend the local church, regardless of whether that church was Lutheran, Reformed, Anglican, or even Catholic. In the West Indies or Greenland, however, there was often no local church for the convert to attend, particularly if the convert was a black slave or an aboriginal. Public worship was something the Brethren themselves had to provide.[28] As was also true of the Methodists, the society came first and the church later.

Wesley's connection with the Brethren dated from his Georgia mission. He had gone to Georgia in 1735 to convert American Indians, but once there, had found himself conscripted to serve as parson to the Anglican congregation in Savannah. His stay in Georgia lasted almost two years. The Moravians had established themselves at Savannah a year before he arrived. They had come to prepare a settlement for the reception of refugees who were fleeing persecution in Silesia. But the migration was diverted and never reached Savannah. For a time, the Moravian settlement was run as an Indian mission but was abandoned in 1740. In Savannah, Wesley and the Moravians lived on intimate terms. Two or three times a day, they met together for prayer, worship, and religious conversation. According to Wesley, he "unbosomed" himself "without reserve." Indeed, the intimacy had begun before Wesley landed. Nitschmann and twenty-six Moravians had taken passage on the same ship as Wesley, who saw in them "men who have left all for their Master, and who have indeed learned of Him, being meek and lowly, dead to the world, full of faith and of the Holy Ghost." Even before the ship had put to sea, Wesley began studying German. "Oh may we be not only of one tongue, but of one mind and of one heart."[29] The study of German continued in Georgia, and Wesley may have come to speak it fluently. In talking with educated Moravians like Böhler, Spangenberg, and Zinzendorf, Latin was the language he preferred. Before his own quarters were ready, Wesley shared lodgings with the Moravians and could observe their "whole behavior. . . . We were in one room with them from morning to night. . . . They were always employed. . . . They walked worthy of the vocation wherewith they were called, and adorned the gospel of our Lord in all things." Emotionally, Wesley came to depend on the spiritual companionship the Brethren provided. "Oh blessed place," he wrote returning to Savannah after a fortnight's absence, "where, having but one end in view, dissembling and fraud are not; but each of us can pour out his heart without fear into his brother's bosom!" When he returned to England in 1738, Wesley was determined to preserve the connection. He arrived in London on a Friday and within a few days had sought out where the Brethren were to be found—at the home of a Dutch merchant. The date contact was resumed is noted "as a day much to be remembered" in Wesley's journal. "I met Peter Böhler, [Georg] Schulius, [Abraham] Richter, and Wensel Neisser, just then landed from Germany." Wesley arranged for them to obtain lodgings near his own. "And from this time I did not willingly lose any opportunity of conversing with them, while I stayed in London."[30]

What is unusual in the relationship is Wesley's docility. By nature, he was the sort of person who liked to lead. In his journals he figures as the guide who directs others on their way to salvation, but with the Moravians, it was they who led and he who followed. Two days after arriving in Georgia, Wesley was submitting to Spangenberg's spiritual direction. "Do you know yourself?" Spangenberg asked. "Have you the witness within yourself? Does the Spirit of God bear witness with your spirit that you are a child of God?" Wesley "knew not what to answer." Spangenberg persisted: "Do you know Jesus Christ?" Wesley: "I know He is the Saviour of the world." Spangenberg: "True . . . but do you know He has saved you?" Wesley: "I hope he has died to save me." Spangenberg: "Do you know yourself?" Wesley said that he did. "But I fear they were vain words. . . . After my answering he gave me several directions, which may the good God who sent him enable me to follow."[31]

The same subordination is evident when Wesley resumed contact with the Brethren in London. "He knew that he did not properly believe in the Saviour, and was willing to be taught," wrote Peter Böhler. Böhler urged Wesley to put aside all his philosophy. "Mi frater, mi frater, excoquenda est ista tua philosophia." He must preach the faith he himself lacked. "Preach faith *till* you have it; and then *because* you have it, you *will* preach faith." Böhler urged him to preach faith to convicts awaiting execution. Böhler "amazed" him "more and more by the account he gave of the fruits of living faith, —the holiness and happiness which he affirmed to attend it." Step by step, Böhler convinced Wesley that saving faith came as a sensible experience, that it entailed a knowledge of forgiveness and reconciliation with God. This faith could be received as an "instantaneous work."

Moravian converts were produced who testified to this experience in their own lives. "Here ended my disputing," Wesley wrote in his journal. "I could now only cry out, 'Lord, help Thou my unbelief!'" This is the first and last time in Wesley's life when he admits to losing an argument.[32] Together, Böhler and Wesley sang the Pietist hymn *Hier legt mein Sinn sich vor dir nieder*, "My soul before Thee prostrate lies." Before the hymn was finished, Böhler tells us that Wesley began to weep and said he was "'. . . now satisfied of what I said of faith, and he would not question any more about it; that he was clearly convinced of the want of it; but how could he help himself, and how could he obtain such faith? . . .'" Böhler encouraged Wesley to hope.

> He wept heartily and bitterly, as I spoke to him on this matter, and (insisted that) I must pray with him. I can say of him, he is truly a poor sinner, and has a contrite heart, hungering after a better righteousness than that which he has till now possessed, even the righteousness of Jesus Christ.

Wesley and Böhler first met on 7 February; they parted on 4 May when Böhler left London to sail to Georgia. "Oh what a work hath God begun, since his coming into England!" Wesley wrote later. "Such an one as shall never come to an end till heaven and earth pass away." Three days later, Wesley received a long letter written in Latin which Böhler had sent from Southampton. "Cave tibi a peccato incredulitatis, et si nondum vicisti illud, fac ut proximo die illud vincas, per sanguinem Jesu Christi" [Beware of the sin of unbelief; and if you have not conquered it yet, see that you conquer it this very day, through the blood of Jesus Christ]. "Ne Differ, quaeso, credere tuum in Jesum Christo" [Delay not, I beseech you, to believe in *your* Jesus Christ].[33]

Wesley's conversion occurred at a devotional meeting held at an address in Aldersgate Street on 24 May. The context of the conversion was pietistic and presumably Moravian. The purpose of the meeting was to hear a reading of Luther's preface to Romans. This was one of the classic texts of German Pietism routinely appealed to to justify the legitimacy of "living faith." It had played a part in the evangelical conversion of August Francke. Wesley had his conversion on cue.[34] It came at the point where Luther wrote of "the change which God works in the heart through faith in Christ." Then, writes Wesley, "I felt my heart strangely warmed. I felt I did trust in Christ alone for salvation; and an assurance was given me that He had taken away *my* sins, even *mine,* and saved *me* from the law of sin and death." Wesley made no secret of what had happened. "I then testified openly to all there what I now first felt in my heart." What he did not feel, however, was a sense of joy. Could this be real faith? "This cannot be faith; for where is thy joy?" Those present dismissed his doubts. The absence of joy was unimportant; what he felt was true faith. "Then was I taught . . . that, as to the transports of joy that usually attend the beginning of" faith, "especially in those who have mourned deeply, God sometimes giveth, sometimes withholdeth them, according to the counsels of His own will." Reassured, Wesley and his friends rushed to share the news with his brother. "Towards ten," Charles wrote, "my brother was brought in triumph by a troop of our friends, and declared, 'I believe.'"[35] Wesley's conversion had taken place under Moravian instruction. The Brethren were the people in his circle who taught that such a conversion was possible, and they were the people who knew what its manifestations ought to be in the heart of the believer. They alone give him advice on what it was he could expect and what he could not. His spiritual dependence on the Brethren is shown by his immediate decision to go to Germany and see Herrnhut and Marienborn for himself.

> I hoped the conversing with those holy men who were themselves living witnesses of the full power of faith, and yet able to bear with those that are weak, would be a means, under God, of so establishing my soul, that I might go on from faith to faith, and "from strength to strength."

Wesley spent four months in Germany and found what he sought. "I continually met with . . . living proofs of the power of faith: persons saved from inward as well as outward sin by 'love of God shed abroad in their hearts,' and from all doubt and fear by the abiding witness of 'the Holy Ghost given unto them.'" Writing to Charles in England, Wesley said that the spirit of the Brethren exceeded his "highest expectations." Young and old, "they breathe nothing but faith and love at all times and in all places." And to Samuel, his older brother: "God has given me at length the desire of my heart. I am with a Church whose conversation is in heaven, in whom is the mind that was in Christ, and who so walk as He walked. . . . O how high and holy a thing Christianity is!"[36]

His zeal for Moravianism represents something unique in Wesley's life. Nothing corresponds to it in his relationship with Dissenter or

Anglican. "A Church whose conversation is in heaven, in whom is the mind that was in Christ, and who so walk as He walked" surpasses anything he ever said even in favor of the Methodists themselves. With no one else do we find the pliancy and receptiveness that he exhibits in his relationship with Spangenberg and Böhler. Methodism emerges in a Moravian context—this is hard to deny. What *is* denied is the importance of the context for the development of Methodism in its defining characteristics. Whatever happened between Wesley and the Brethren, its effect is represented as something short term and marginal in its importance to the interpretation of Methodism. Wesley's Moravian conversion in 1738 is seen by Clifford Towlson as a response to "an emotional impulse." It is not to be understood as "intellectual assent" to any truth that is doctrinally distinctive. What impressed Wesley most "was not so much the Christianity which the Brethren preached as the Christianity which they lived." For Michael Watts, the Moravian phase represents an aberration in the evolution of Wesley's thought. "Once the example of the Moravians and the writings of Luther had served their purposes, they . . . were set aside and the earlier pre-conversion influences reasserted themselves."[37]

The first historian of Methodism to dispute the importance of the Moravians is, of course, John Wesley. In the 1739 edition of the Georgia journal, he testified to the power and mercy of God, who "hath opened me a door into the whole Moravian Church." In later editions, the "whole Moravian Church" becomes merely the "whole Church." The early journals reveal a debt to the Brethren that Wesley sought to minimize. In his *Short History of Methodism,* published in 1765, he makes no reference to the Moravians. Methodism commences in Oxford in the 1720s. Georgia is mentioned, but nothing is said of his intimacy with Spangenberg and the other Moravian missionaries. Nor is anything written about his association with the Moravians in London; nor about his Aldersgate experience. In the *Short History,* as in his journals, Wesley stresses the importance of saving faith but makes no reference to the Brethren, from whom he had learned about it.[38] In a brief survey of Methodism written in 1777, the connection was again suppressed. In this version of the story, Methodism derives from its origins in Oxford and Georgia; it owes nothing to Moravian influence. "Methodism, so-called, is the old religion, the religion of the Bible, the religion of the primitive church, the religion of the Church of England."[39] In 1781, Wesley published a fuller, more detailed history: *A Short History of the People Called Methodists*. Here, the Brethren are mentioned somewhat incidentally; lest we exaggerate their importance, though, we are reminded of Methodism's first foundation in Oxford and Georgia.[40] In *Thoughts on Methodism,* written in 1786, the Brethren are once again omitted from the record.[41] The suppression of the Moravians by Wesley owes nothing to the vanity or forgetfulness of old age; it begins shortly after the break in 1740. In 1743, he published the *General Rules of the United Societies,* in which Methodism is said to have begun in London in 1739, when Wesley agreed to direct penitents "who appeared to be deeply convinced of sin, and earnestly groaning for redemption." From this association the Methodist movement arose. No reference is made to the Moravians. And no less significant, no reference is made to Oxford. Methodism emerged without antecedents either in Germany or England. It just happens.[42] In 1748, he published the *Plain Account of the People Called Methodists,* which is longer and more detailed. Again, Methodism starts in London 1739, with no reference made to Oxford. Methodism begins in Wesley's Moravian period, but the Moravians are forgotten.[43] Clearly, the association with the Moravians is something in Wesley's past, something he preferred not to talk about. Had Wesley postponed publication of his early journals, the importance of the Moravians might possibly have been forgotten. Fortunately, the volume that covers the Georgia mission came out in 1739, and the volume covering the Aldersgate conversion and the visit to Herrnhut and Marienborn, in September 1740. The first volume was published before the quarrel with the Brethren had erupted, and the second while it was in progress. In the second volume, Wesley prints numerous statements made by the Brethren in Germany, which tend to support his conception of saving faith. The work may have been published to demonstrate that Wesley, and not his opponents, were more faithful to real Moravianism. Whatever his motive may have been, too much of the story had been given to the public for Wesley to deny the reality of the connection as a historical event. All he could do was pretend it was an event that did not matter.[44]

2

Conviction

METHODISM DID NOT DEFINE ITSELF IN TERMS OF DOCTRINAL ORTHODOXY. JOHN Wesley never worked out a systematic theology, nor did he formulate a distinctive creed. Credal statements he possibly disliked. In the edition of the *Book of Common Prayer* he issued for use in America, the Athanasian Creed was left out. At a time when orthodox christology was threatened by Unitarianism, the omission is significant. Although Wesley was no Unitarian, Unitarianism was not something he wanted condemned in public worship week after week. In a sense, orthodoxy did not matter. "I make no opinion the term of union with any man. I think, and let think. What I want is holiness of heart and life." In practice, he did quarrel over doctrine; when he broke with his opponents, however, it was their bad conduct, and not their bad doctrine, that he chose to complain about. "I can have no connexion with those who will be contentious. These I reject, not for their opinion, but for their sin; for their unchristian temper, and unchristian practice."[1] In the *Character of a Methodist,* he denied that Methodism possessed a credal or theological identity:

> The distinguishing marks of a Methodist are not his opinions of any sort. His assenting to this or that scheme of religion, his embracing any particular set of notions, his espousing the judgment of one man or another, are all quite wide of the point. Whosoever, therefore, imagines that a Methodist is a man of such or such an opinion, is grossly ignorant of the whole affair; he mistakes the truth totally.[2]

Membership in the society was consistent with membership in any church. No candidate was asked to subscribe to a set of principles. He did not even have to profess Christianity. All that is required is a wish to flee "the wrath to come." There is, Wesley wrote, "no other religious society under heaven which requires nothing of men in order to their admission into it but a desire to save their souls."[3] On

31

admission, the member did not cease to attend his own church for Sunday service. "The Presbyterian may be a Presbyterian still; the Independent or Anabaptist use his own mode of worship. So may the Quaker; and none will contend with him about it."[4]

The Brethren exhibit a similar Latitudinarianism in the matter of true doctrine. In their own church—that is, the church they had reinvented with David Nitschmann's consecration as a Moravian bishop in 1735—diversity was encouraged. Members were registered according to their *tropus* (Latin, meaning a figure of speech); in the Moravian context, it refers to the denomination the member belonged to before joining. The word implies that the differences between churches correspond to the differences in figures of speech that refer to the same thing. It is the reference that matters, not the diversity of terms in which it is stated; differences do not matter. Joining the Society did not mean the member had to disown the church he already belonged to. In practice, only three *tropi* were instituted: Lutheran, Reformed, and Moravian. The Moravian was the smallest of the three, membership being restricted to refugees who could claim some affiliation with the real Moravian church.[5] For practical reasons, Zinzendorf stopped at three. In principle, there was no objection to the institution of *tropi* for Anglican, Mennonite, and Catholic recruits. In expectation of a Jewish conversion, Zinzendorf considered a *tropus* for those who wished to observe Jewish law and ritual.[6] Friendly clergy were invited to preside over a *tropus* and to represent its point of view at Society conferences. Christian Cochius, court preacher at Potsdam, and, on his death, Thomas Wilson, bishop of Sodor and Man, represented the Reformed *tropus;* Johannes Hermann, the court preacher at Dresden, represented the Lutheran *tropus.* This was an honor the Brethren perhaps were more eager to confer than the nominees were to accept. Cochius and Wilson were appointed only after Zinzendorf had failed to find a suitable Calvinist in the Netherlands. Increasingly, the Brethren had to recruit the *tropus* presidents from their own ranks.[7] The *tropus* worked as a unit of registration, and little else. It was not meant to segregate members for purposes of administration and worship. Even as a unit of registration, however, it illustrates how little confessional uniformity mattered. On joining the Society, the new member did not cease to be a Lutheran or a Calvinist or a Moravian. What divided denominations was less important than what united them. All denominations were legitimate; diversity in religion reflected nothing more than a diversity in human temperament and historical background. Believers were to be found everywhere and in all churches. As believers, it was their duty to remain faithful to the church in which providence had placed them. Faults in doctrine and discipline were to be submitted to patiently. "What cannot be changed and God suffers, the believer will accept also with forbearance," wrote Spangenberg.[8] All denominations were valid and, in their diversity, were of benefit to their members. "Each church," wrote Ludwig Schrautenbach, "receives a precious fund of truth, with which its members work out their salvation." The church existed for the sake of itself and for the sake of all mankind. "We can waste nothing. The truth a church is entrusted with, must be defended and proclaimed to everyone." Diversity was not something that Christians had to regret or condemn. "No case could be made for merging all religions into a single system."[9] Diversity was good in itself; it was also consistent with membership in the Moravian connection.

Brethren and Methodists alike distinguished between faith as assent to doctrine and faith as the conscious transformation of the mind. In the first sense, it was unimportant; in the second, it was not. Religion did not consist in orthodoxy or right opinion. "A man may be orthodox in every point," wrote Wesley.

> He may think justly concerning the incarnation of our Lord, concerning the ever-blessed Trinity, and every other doctrine contained in the oracles of God; he may assent to all the three Creeds . . . and yet it is possible he may have no religion at all, no more than a Jew, Turk, or Pagan.

Faith, in this sense, was something even devils might possess. Devils knew that Jesus was born of a virgin, that He worked miracles, revealed his divinity, died for our sins, rose from the dead, ascended to heaven, and in the end would return to judge the world. "This the devils believe; and so they believe all that is written in the Old and New Testament: And yet still, for all this faith, they are but devils; they remain still in their damnable estate, lacking the true Christian faith."[10] For Wesley, faith was a miraculous event worked by the Holy Ghost in the believer's heart. The possession of faith entailed the believer's perception of his status. "It is a divine evidence . . . that the Son of God hath loved *me,* and given himself for *me;* and that I, even I, am now reconciled to God by the blood of the cross." To this extent, faith was truth that the believer knew about himself; and, because it presupposed the intervention of the Holy Ghost, it differed from other kinds of knowledge. It was not knowledge the believer could be reasoned into, nor was it knowledge that much depended on the believer's orthodoxy. "I hold a divine evidence or conviction that Christ loved *me* and gave Himself for *me* is essential to if not the very essence of justifying faith." What the believer knew to be true found its confirmation in the testimony of his own heart.

> So Christianity tells me; and So I find it, may every real Christian say. I now am assured that these things are so: I experience them in my own breast. What Christianity (considered as a doctrine) promised is accomplished in my soul. And Christianity, considered as an inward principle, is the completion of all those promises.[11]

Wesley's idea of faith is sometimes seen as deriving from a Puritan influence working on him through his family. Both parents had been raised as Dissenters. Before turning Anglican, his father studied for the ministry as an Independent. His mother Susanna was the daughter of Samuel Annesley, a Puritan divine who had been ejected from his living in 1662. John Newton tells us that as a child at Epworth, Wesley absorbed Puritan influence "with his mother's milk."[12] In some respects, his conception of faith resembles the assurance of grace and salvation believers are encouraged to hope for in the Westminster Confession: "an infallible assurance of faith, founded upon the divine truth of the promises of salvation . . . the testimony of the Spirit of adoption witnessing with our spirits that we are the children of God." The correspondence between the two conceptions of faith is imperfect, however. For Wesley, consciousness of pardon is essential to faith. In the Westminster Confession, it is not. In Methodism, knowledge of forgiveness comes to all who believe; not so in the Westminster Confession. "This infallible assurance doth not so belong to the essence of faith, but that a true believer may wait long, and conflict with many difficulties before he be partaker of it."[13] Whatever Wesley's connection with Puritanism may have been, it did not run through his family. His mother spoke of faith as assent to truth and not as consciousness of pardon and a disposition of the heart: "The true measure of faith is the authority of the revealer," she wrote in 1725. "Divine faith is an assent to whatever God has revealed to us, because he has revealed it. And this is that virtue of faith which is one of the . . . conditions of our salvation by Jesus Christ." In defense of this definition, Wesley's mother invoked the somewhat unpuritanical authority of Bishop Pearson's *Exposition of the Creed*

(1659).[14] By Methodist standards, faith in these terms was neither saving nor living faith; it was a faith that could be entertained by devils or, at best, by servants of God. What is missing is the critical consciousness of pardon that identified it as the faith received by the child of God. Wesley's mother knew nothing of faith in this sense. "She had scarce heard such a thing mentioned as having forgiveness of sins now," Wesley wrote; "or God's Spirit bearing witness with our spirit; much less did she imagine this was the common privilege of all true believers." Nor was it something she could remember her father preaching about: "No, not once—explicitly . . . whence she supposed he looked upon it as the peculiar blessing of a few, not as promised to all the people of God."[15] Wesley's idea of faith came from the Moravians, not the Puritans.

The distinction between saving faith and intellectual assent to the truths of religion was what Lutheran Pietism had insisted on in its quarrel with Lutheran Orthodoxy. In *Pia desideria,* Philip Spener appealed to 1 Corinthians 2:4. "And my speech and my preaching *was* not with enticing words of man's wisdom, but in demonstration of the Spirit and of power." Christian faith presupposed more than a reasonable assent to Christian truth. "Zu diesem gehöret ein mehreres." A new disposition had to be aroused. The believer must feel in his heart a conscious yearning to serve God and magnify his glory. Merely knowing what was true was not enough.[16] In the case of his own conversion, August Francke thought of knowledge as if it were an impediment to the acquisition of faith. "I could explain what belief, regeneration and justification were, but none of these things were evident in my own heart." Real faith manifested itself in the believer's power to perform the will of God. If a choice had to be made between knowledge and power, then power was to be preferred. "It is better knowing little to apply it with energy than knowing much to let it languish unused."[17] In denying that faith was intellectual assent, the Pietists could invoke the authority of Luther himself. In this sense, it was they who were orthodox, and their opponents who were not. The text appealed to was Luther's preface to Romans and the critical passage, the same that Wesley refers to in the account of his Aldersgate conversion.

> Faith . . . is something that God effects in us. It changes us and we are reborn from God. . . . Faith puts the old Adam to death and makes us quite different men in heart, in mind, and in all our powers. . . . O, when

it comes to faith, what a living, creative, active, powerful thing it is. . . .
Faith is a living and unshakable confidence, a belief in the grace of God
so assured that a man would die a thousand deaths for its sake. This
kind of confidence in God's grace, this sort of knowledge of it, makes
us joyful and high-spirited, and eager in our relations with God and with
all mankind.[18]

This is the definition of faith that is assumed by Pietists. It is cited
by Spener, Francke, and Zinzendorf. It has been called the Magna
Carta of German Pietism.[19] By appealing to it, Pietists could insist
on the need for a conscious conversion and still claim to be good
Lutherans.

Whether it was Pietism or Orthodoxy that better reflected what
Luther meant need not be decided here. Both sides agreed on salvation by faith; how salvation by faith *worked* was the question that
divided them. In Orthodoxy, faith effects our pardon; in Pietism, it
effects rebirth. No doubt, this statement oversimplifies the controversy. Pardon was not denied by the Pietists, nor rebirth by the Orthodox. It was a matter of emphasis or priority. Which came first? Which
was more important? Which the cause and which the effect? Orthodoxy saw faith as an event that decides our legal relationship with
God. Through faith, we are justified; our sins are forgiven. But in
believing, nothing in us is changed; we do not cease to be sinners;
and we can claim no merit apart from our belief. In Pietism, we are
changed. We are born again, and in our rebirth we are freed from
the power of sin. We acquire a new nature, and with this new nature
we may grow in righteousness.[20] In Orthodoxy, justification is all that
matters; in Pietism, justification figures as a stage in a process of
transformation. Associating belief and rebirth, the Pietist expected
faith to manifest itself empirically. Like Wesley, Francke felt the truth
he had discovered. "With the wave of a hand, all my doubt vanished.
In my heart I was assured of the grace of God in Jesus Christ . . . My
heart was freed at once of sadness and anxiety. A flood of joy poured
over me . . ."[21] In Pietism, emphasis on faith tends to be threatened
by emphasis on real transformation. Rebirth might commence before
faith is clearly apprehended; once it is apprehended, the believer is
encouraged to grow in sanctity. In this sense, sanctity competes with
justification. The possibility of perfection in sanctity was taught by
Spener and Francke. True Christianity entailed progress in righteousness. In God's kingdom, Francke wrote, "we go from one level to the
next and never stop. Standing still we lose what we have and fall

into the clutches of the enemy." In Christianity, there are degrees. "When one is mastered, we can proceed more confidently to the next and in the end we may reach the goal set before us."[22] The dispute between Orthodox and Pietists over sanctification reproduces itself in the dispute between Methodists and Moravians in the Fetter Lane schism. In the autumn of 1741, Wesley and Zinzendorf met to discuss their differences. The meeting turned into debate over sanctification. Wesley argued for rebirth and a holiness that was real, Zinzendorf for justification and a holiness that was only imputed. Zinzendorf condemned real holiness as the error of errors:

> I pursue it everywhere with fire and sword! . . . Christ is our only perfection. Whoever affirms inherent perfection denies Christ. . . . All Christian perfection is simply faith in Christ's blood. Christian perfection is entirely imputed, not inherent. We are perfect in Christ; never perfect in ourselves.

Justification was everything; in his justification, the believer attained the only kind of sanctity he could expect. "From the moment one is justified, he is entirely sanctified. Thereafter till death he is neither more holy nor less holy. . . . The event of sanctification and justification is completed in an instant. Thereafter, it neither increases nor decreases."[23]

Sanctification as a topic in dispute emerges late in the history of the schism. The dispute began in disagreement over the need for converts to feel contrition before attaining faith. Contrition and sanctification are topics related in logic. In both, assumptions are made about the status of the believer: in sanctification, about the believer's status after he or she believes; and in contrition before. In both cases, the dispute turns on how salvation is thought of. If it is primarily regeneration, then contrition and sanctification may be seen as stages in a process of development; if it is forgiveness, it may take effect without being preceded by contrition or followed by sanctification.

The Fetter Lane dispute over contrition duplicated the Orthodox-Pietist dispute in Germany. In classic Pietism, the believer's conversion commenced with a penitential struggle, *Bußkampf.* Saving faith was not something that could be proceeded to straightaway. Before we can be saved, we must be convinced of our own sinfulness, of our utter dependence on the grace of God. Indeed, the first stirrings of faith assured the believer of nothing but his damnation and hopelessness. Faith begins with despair. In Francke's conception of the *Bußkampf*, we may begin by trying to lead better lives. But our plans miscarry. We are too weak and the power of sin too strong. "We sink ever deeper into the filth of iniquity," he said. In our impotence and dejection, we may feel the first stirrings of a feeble faith. It manifests itself as real contrition, as a "Zuschlagung des Hertzens." With this faith, we may come to yearn for the forgiveness of our sins, but this is not the faith that will save us or that will effect our rebirth. We must continue to struggle, all the while encouraged by hope and assailed by terror. Our mental distress corresponds to the physical sufferings of natural birth. How long it lasts depends on God's will. We must persevere in the struggle. "Gleichwie es mit der Geburts-Stunde hergehet es will die Zeit abwartet seyn, ehe mögen die Schmertzen nicht auffhören." It is in the extremity of our terror and despair, and only then, that the force of the Gospel promise takes effect. Only when we are convinced of our sinfulness and help-lessness can we begin to apply to ourselves the hope offered by the Gospels. In Pietist terminology, this is the breakthrough, or *Durch-bruch*. By the grace of God, we have been brought to the point of complete despair, and again through the grace of God we come to believe in our salvation through the sacrifice of Christ. This is saving faith. With it, our terror ends and we feel a sense of deliverance. We know that our sins are forgiven. As children of God, we have acquired in ourselves a new power to resist temptation and sin. The ordeal of the *Bußkampf* is not something the convert can hope to avoid. "There is no other way," Francke wrote. "Twist and turn as much as you like. If you wish to become the temple of God and his holy Spirit, then you must ask him first that you be convinced of your wretch-edness and corruption." A broken, contrite heart was the proper *Werckstatt* in which Christ was to be glorified. If the contrition or conviction of sin or repentance does not manifest itself in the heart of the sinner, "then nothing can be understood about the spirit of God and its power." No *Bußkampf*, no saving faith.[24]

As a pupil of Francke's, Zinzendorf had been introduced to *Buß-kampf* piety at Halle. It was Halle that taught him, he complained, to subordinate the Gospels to the law. "Erst war Moses, der gab die 10 Gebote, darnach kam der Heiland, da glaubte man ans Evangelium." *Bußkampf* exercises were "a tedious and futile struggle" in which he persevered "again and again." In its classic form, the *Durchbruch* was something Zinzendorf never attained. In 1729, he is still lamenting his fallen state. He could think of himself as one of God's servants but not as a son. In his heart, he felt no assurance of his adoption. This failure, more than any theological consideration, perhaps explains his final rejection of *Bußkampf* piety; but, in the early days of Herrnhut's foundation, Zinzendorf was committed to the *Bußkampf* and promoted it with vigor.[25] In a children's catechism published in 1723, he urges the reader to start with penitence:

> Remember, you are disobedient, wanton; you never tell the truth, you are greedy and want more, even though you have enough. . . . you ought to be punished; and it would serve you right, if God cast you into the fires of Hell.

In 1727, *Bußkampf* conversion was recommended to a friend. "The proper way to the kingdom of God for all men, is that they come to mourn and acknowledge their wretchedness. The things of this world must be shunned . . . and the viciousness in the heart exposed."[26] Religious instruction at Herrnhut was established according to *Bußkampf* principles. In accordance with their spiritual progress, people were divided into classes: separate classes were instituted for the *converted*, the *awakened*, and the *dead*. Sometimes the classes were identified by different names. We hear also of *young men, children*, and *beginners*. A class of *children* might consist entirely of adults and a class of *young men* entirely of women. It was the spiritual, not the natural status, of the members that was referred to.[27] On the day classes were assigned, the members of the congregation examined themselves and declared the state of their soul: "wie es mit dem Heiland stünde." "Whoever was troubled, confessed it," wrote Spangenberg. The unbeliever said, "I am still unconverted"; the stubborn admitted their stubbornness. Those who were converted said that they loved their Savior. Everyone was assigned to the proper class, "nach der Verschiedenheit der Herzenssituation." Wesley reports the details of *Bußkampf* segregation in his journal record of a visit to Herrnhut in 1738: "The members of the Church are divided . . . with regard to their proficiency in the knowledge of God. Some are dead, some quickened by the spirit of God." Penitents caught up in the travails of conversion might be more precisely classified. "Of these," Wesley reports, "some are untractable, some diligent, some zealous, burning with their first love; some babes, and some young men."[28] Class leaders met regularly and discussed the progress of their penitents. These could be rated as cooperative *(willig)*, frustrated *(verstockt)*, lifeless *(tot)*, proceeding toward grace *(auf Gnade gehend)*, earnest *(innig)*, fervent *(brünstig)*, fearful *(bänglich)*, cheerful *(munter)*, alert *(wachsam)*, drifting *(trudelhaft)*, perplexed *(confus)*, fastidious *(scrupulös)*, strong *(kräftig)*, or devastated *(niedergeschlagen)*.[29] To this extent were degrees of faith recognized in early Herrnhut.

The idea of conversion as a process beginning with the conviction of sin belonged to a phase of Moravian history that did not persist. In the recollections of Spangenberg and David Cranz, the *Bußkampf* came to be thought of as a legalistic, unevangelical institution inconsistent with the real truth Moravians taught. The real truth was their *Versöhnungslehre,* or doctrine of atonement. As they came to see themselves, it was this doctrine that gave them their special identity. "It is this, and this only that defines the Brethren," wrote Ludwig Schrautenbach.[30] What this doctrine asserted was the radical significance of Jesus' atonement on the cross. That Jesus died for us constitutes the totality of Christian truth. "For a wretched worm like me, he shed his blood," said Zinzendorf; "das ist die ganze Herzenstheologie." This is the "one and only truth" the Moravians preached. "It is our panacea against everything that is wrong in thought and deed. It will be so for ever."[31] For Zinzendorf, the reality of the atonement became the first fact of Christianity, to which everything else was subordinated. Indeed, any truth it did not imply might be ignored. "Was ich nicht aus ihr deduciren könte," said Zinzendorf, "gleich wegwerfen wolte."[32] In principle, the doctrine asserted nothing that Pietists or Methodists might object to. As Protestants, they too taught the sufficiency of Christ's atonement. No one can save himself by his own merits. What caused the trouble was the way in which Moravians applied the doctrine in the guidance of converts. If our redemption by Christ is the "first fact" of Christianity, they believed, it is in the recognition of this fact that conversion must begin and end. As a conversion strategy, the *Bußkampf* directs one's attention to the wrong thing—that is, to the law of God and our guilt under it, not to the fact of our redemption. To effect conversion, we must begin with the knowledge of Christ's sacrifice, not with the knowledge of our own guilt. We must start with the Gospel, not the law. In the *Bußkampf,* conversion begins with the hatred of sin. It begins with terror and fear. In the conversion implied in the *Versöhnungslehre,* we start with knowledge of our redemption, only afterward feeling sorrow for our sins. From the suffering of Jesus on the cross, it is seen how gravely we have offended God. We know that we once were damned only when we have learned of our forgiveness. We experience contrition only after we learn that our sins no longer matter. Sorrow is the result of our salvation—not, in any sense, its precondition.[33] The *Bußkampf* conversion commences in fear and proceeds with hesitation and doubt; the Moravian conversion starts joyful and remains confident. The *Bußkampf* conversion is a gradual process in which the believer progresses from one stage to the next. The Moravian conversion is an abrupt change from not having faith to possessing faith. Whoever lacks faith struggles against sin in vain; whoever has faith struggles no more. With faith comes power over sin; further struggle is needless. The gift of faith is immediate. There are no degrees, no gracious preliminaries or stages in which the unbeliever may imagine that he possesses the very thing he lacks. The Lord does not expect us to prepare ourselves for his kingdom, said Zinzendorf. "He is mighty enough, and close enough to unlock our hearts and reveal himself simply and effectively."[34] The Pietists looked on *Bußkampf* travail as a manifestation of grace that the penitent has received in some form or some degree. The penitent may not yet believe and may not yet be saved, but in his despair may be discerned the promise of hope to come. In their rejection of the *Bußkampf*, Moravians did not deny the reality of contrition. Christians did experience conviction of sin. This conviction might come before, after, or during conversion. What was objected to was the insistence on *prior* contrition.[35] In this sense, the *Bußkampf* did not work—or did not work very well. Zinzendorf compared it to eating soup with a sieve. Those who will not believe the Gospel may turn to the law. "They must trouble and torment themselves until the Holy Spirit takes pity and Jesus is revealed to their hearts."[36]

Zinzendorf's private adoption of the *Versöhnungslehre* dates from 1734, six years before the Fetter Lane schism and one year before Wesley made contact with the Moravians in Georgia.[37] The new doctrine was not taught in public before the winter of 1738, when Zinzendorf delivered a series of sermons in Berlin. The first printed statement is made in 1739, with the publication of Zinzendorf's *Sonderbare Gespräche*. No *Bußkampf* was necessary. No rules or patterns or methods can be prescribed for conversion. No prior disposition of the heart can be insisted upon. No sinner must struggle before faith is granted, and he is reborn of the Holy Spirit. The only *Bußkampf* required was performed by Jesus on the cross. In contemplating our iniquity, the only sin we need worry about is the sin of unbelief.[38] Among the Brethren themselves, the reception of the new doctrine was a gradual process which did not take place without resistance and hesitation. In Herrnhut, *Bußkampf* piety persisted long after it had been abandoned by Zinzendorf in theory. Having been exiled from Saxony, Zinzendorf could not administer Herrnhut directly. In the Herrnhut school as late as 1738, children were still rated on their progress in the *Bußkampf*. In Wesley's journal, it is implied—perhaps inaccurately—that as late as 1739, adults at Herrnhut were still sorted into *Bußkampf* bands. Formal adoption by the Moravian brotherhood of the *Versöhnungslehre* in its entirety does not occur until 1740, the year of the Fetter Lane schism.[39] As a Moravian institution, the *Bußkampf* held out longest in areas remote from Zinzendorf's immediate supervision. In St. Thomas in the West Indies, it persisted until 1740, when Christian Israel was sent to propagate the new doctrine. The blacks, Israel wrote, were just as precise and methodical as the Brethren had been in the practice of *Bußkampf* discipline: "First they are awakened and come to know their wicked state. Then they scream and sob for mercy until a comfort is sensed and they can feel their belief in the wounds of Jesus." What Israel describes in St. Thomas duplicates what Molther encountered the same time at Fetter Lane: manifestations of the conviction that the Brethren had previously taught their adherents to seek. Israel and Molther disparaged the old piety from the perspective of the new. *Bußkampf* conversions had also been encouraged in Greenland. In his *Historical Sketches of the Missions of the United Brethren* (1817), John Holmes describes an instance dating from 1738. The Brethren endeavored to make the convert "attentive to the state of his soul. At first, their instructions seemed unavailing, but by degrees they discovered some relentings of heart, and conviction of sin; and when they prayed with him tears generally started into his eyes." It was Zinzendorf's complaint that the mission, in its reports, said nothing of the *Verdienst Christi*. Conversions were frustrated by the *gottlose Methode* the Brethren employed. "It is worth our while, to show our disapproval here."[40] The *Bußkampf* in Greenland held out until 1740. According to Holmes, that year the missionaries were at last won over and persuaded

in the literal sense of the words, to preach Christ and Him crucified, without first 'laying the foundation of repentance from dead works, and faith towards God.' No sooner did they declare unto the Greenlanders 'the word of reconciliation' in its native simplicity, than they beheld its converting and saving power.

The *Versöhnungslehre* worked where the *Bußkampf* had failed.

A sure foundation being thus laid in the knowledge of a crucified Redeemer, the missionaries soon found that this supplied their . . . converts with a powerful motive to the abhorrence of sin, . . . in a manner far more correct and influential, than they could ever have attained, had they persevered in their first mode of instruction.[41]

The first evidence from Georgia that Moravians expounded the *Versöhnungslehre* also dates from 1740, two years after Wesley had returned to England. A conversation with the Lutheran ministers at Ebenezer is reported by John Hagen:

One thing in particular they asked me about, which they found hard to understand. This is that if we believe in Jesus, we are freed from the power of sin, that we do not have to struggle and fight against it. . . . This is not impossible for the one who has come to know about the mystery of the cross and the death of our Lord. . . . Once we turn to the cross and discover its power, the substance of sin is totally destroyed.

The Lutherans, good Pietists and members of the Halle connection, understood this as antinomianism: The Moravian brotherhood stood on a dangerous ground, *auf einem hohen Felsen.* Yes, said Hagen, "but we stand by Jesus Christ our king, and there we always mean to stay."[42] Peter Böhler may have introduced the new doctrine when he got to Georgia in 1738, but before 1738, nothing was known of it. The Moravianism Wesley learned about in Georgia was standard German Pietism. Like Herrnhut, it presupposed a conversion that progressed in degrees, starting with contrition and proceeding to faith and the forgiveness of sins. Before he joined the Moravians, Spangenberg had taken part in a Pietist revival at the University of Jena. In the revival, what had been preached was the law, not the Gospel: "We were urged to repent and experience sorrow and regret," Spangenberg said. "What was taught was that each of us should come to know the kind of terror that a criminal feels when he is led to judgement." His background in Pietism was something Spangenberg found difficult to renounce. Spangenberg's own introduction to the *Versöhnungslehre* did not take place until after he had left Georgia.

"Returning from America in 1739, I found that the brethren had received salvation in the blood of the lamb. During my absence they had grown beyond measure in the knowledge of God's martyrdom, upon which all salvation depends."[43] From Spangenberg, Wesley was told nothing about blood and wounds, nor was he ever urged to proceed to faith. Instead, Wesley was asked to examine himself: "Do you know yourself? Have you the witness within yourself?" He was told that there were degrees of faith and the passage to it was gradual. Wesley himself possessed a degree of faith: "Habes fidem, sed exiguam." In coming to faith, the Christian was assisted by outward means. One of these outward means was self-examination. Others were reading and hearing scripture, fasting, and fervent prayer. Holy communion was a means of grace; faith was perfected by good works. Conversion was something perceptible in the mind. It was like passing from "darkness unto light." It could be worked in a moment, "but the passage itself is gradual."[44] Utterly absent is any reference to the martyrdom of God, "upon which all salvation depends." Nothing was said of blood and wounds. What Wesley heard about Herrnhut referred to Herrnhut in its Pietist phase. There, converts were first urged to think of themselves and to examine the condition of their souls. Once they were awakened by the power of the word, they were guided from one stage of conversion to the other: "damit sie in der Gnade von einem Grade zum andern fortschritten." Wesley's instruction in Georgia stands in contrast to what he learned from Peter Böhler in London. In London, there is one primary injunction: *believe*. There is also only one primary sin: unbelief. Through the blood of Jesus, this sin is conquered. Belief must come before everything else; everything else will come after belief." Crede igitur. . . . Admonish one another to believe, and then to walk *circumspectly* in the sight of God, to fight *lawfully* against the devil and the world, and to crucify and to tread all sin under your feet."[45] Possibly, Wesley did not perceive the difference. In Savannah, he had been instructed in *Bußkampf* discipline and in London in the *Versöhnungslehre*.

Wesley's response to Böhler must be seen as the culmination of a *Bußkampf* process that had begun in Georgia. His parishioners there were encouraged to examine themselves. In his diary, Wesley wrote down the names of penitents who were *affected* or *serious* and those who were *convinced*, that is laboring under the conviction of sin.[46] March 17, 1736: "Appee *in Orco*, but hopes"; April 21: "Ingham dead! O Jesus!"; May 12: "John Chapman half convinced."[47] On 11 July 1736, he preached a conviction sermon on John 8:46 to a large congregation, "whom I endeavored to convince of unbelief."[48] Wesley's own progress in the *Bußkampf* is not easy to reconstruct. That he was engaged in regular self-examination can be seen from his diary. Every day, he rated himself under an entry for *Grace.* Friday, October 31, 1735: "Grace: Renewed resolutions. Lively zeal." The entry noted the times and the intensity of the manifestations. The latter was shown by an ascending numerical scale. Thus, the entry for May 3, 1736 reads: "Grace: 7 rating once [4 to 5 P.M.]; 6 eight times [4 to 7, 9 to 10 A.M., 5 to 9 P.M.]." This was not merely a record of temperamental blessings. Wesley was committed to the *Bußkampf.* On May 8, 1736, September 29, and October 1, manifestations of *convincing* grace are reported.[49] On April 11, we find "Grace: Something like faith. + [noon to 1 P.M.]." The last entry under the heading of *grace* was made on July 21, 1737. "Grace: 6 rating sixteen times; 5 once [twice, noon to 1, 8 to 9 P.M.]"[50] Fortunately, his progress in self-examination can be followed in the text of the published journals. On the voyage back to England, Wesley experienced the spiritual crisis that *Bußkampf* discipline taught the penitent to expect and, in a sense, even to hope for. This is the real recognition that faith was lacking and that nothing but damnation was deserved. "By the most infallible of proofs, inward feeling I am convinced . . . of unbelief; having no such faith in Christ as will prevent my heart from being troubled; which it could not be, if I believed in God, and rightly believed also in Him." In the self-condemnation, he lists the sins of pride, irrecollection, levity, and luxuriancy of spirit. "Lord save, or I perish! Save me . . . by such a faith as implies peace in life and in death." In his despair, relief was found in preaching the word of God to his shipmates. Was the relief legitimate or illegitimate?

> I am sensible one who thinks the being *in orco,* as they phrase it, an indispensable preparative for being a Christian, would say I had better have continued in that state; and that this unseasonable relief was a curse, not blessing. Nay, but who art thou, O man, who in favour of a wretched hypothesis, thus blasphemest the good gift of God?

The relief did not persist and the terror returned stronger than ever. "I, who went to America to convert others, was never myself converted to God." Wesley's only faith was a "rational conviction" that Christianity was true, but this was not the faith that saves. He was

damned. "My whole heart is 'altogether corrupt and abominable' . . .
I am a 'child of wrath' an heir of hell." His works and righteousness
counted for nothing. The "sentence of death" lay in his heart. "I have
no hope, but that of being justified freely, 'through the redemption
that is in Jesus.'" But this was to be obtained only through faith, a
faith he did not possess. "The faith I want is 'a sure trust and confidence in God, that, through the merits of Christ, my sins are forgiven,
and I reconciled to the favour of God.'" He lacked the faith recommended by Saint Paul:

> I want that faith which none can have without knowing that he hath it
> . . . for whosoever hath it, is "freed from sin," the whole "body of sin is
> destroyed" in him: he is freed from fear, "having peace with God through
> Christ." . . . And he is freed from doubt, "having the love of God shed
> abroad in his heart, through the Holy Ghost which is given unto him";
> which "Spirit itself beareth witness with his spirit, that he is a child
> of God."

Wesley later described the *Bußkampf* stage of his conversion as a
period of struggle and conflict: "In this vile abject state of bondage
to sin, I was indeed fighting continually, but not conquering. Before,
I had willingly served sin: now it was unwillingly; but still I served
it." In the classic *Bußkampf* pattern, false victories were won and
followed by more terrible defeats. "I fell, and rose, and fell again."
In the struggle gracious intimations might be received. "Sometimes
I was overcome and in heaviness: sometimes I overcame, and was
in joy." For, "as in the former state I had some foretastes of the terrors
of the law; so had I in this, of the comforts of the gospel. During this
whole struggle between nature and grace, which had now continued
above ten years, I had many remarkable returns to prayer. . . . I had
many sensible comforts." Such comforts were "short anticipations
of the life of faith," but Wesley still labored "under the law," not
"under grace." He was "only striving with, not freed from sin." He
lacked the witness of the Spirit and knew not how to obtain it. "For
I 'sought it not by faith, but as it were by the works of the law.'"[51]
Belief was something Böhler urged on Wesley as an alternative to
the *Bußkampf*. In Wesley's mind, it was understood as the climax in
which the *Bußkampf* culminated; that this was not the case was
discovered only when Wesley got to Herrnhut. There, in a sermon
preached by Christian David, he heard about the *Versöhnungslehre*.
It was David who had led the original migration from Moravia to

Zinzendorf's estate. He was also the founder of the Greenland mission. "The sermon," said Wesley, "made such an impression upon me that when I went home I could not but write down the substance of it." In the published journals, Wesley's summary runs to a page and a half. What reconciles us to God, "wholly and solely" the "blood of Christ." We may grieve for our sins. But this contributes nothing to our justification. "Nay, observe . . . . that it may hinder your justification; that is, if you build anything upon it; if you think, I must be *so or so* contrite, I must grieve *more* before I can be justified." The impediment of our own contrition must be removed, before the right foundation for faith can be laid. "The right foundation is, not *your* contrition . . . not *your* righteousness, nothing of *your own*, nothing that is wrought *in you* by the Holy Ghost." It is "something *without you* viz. the righteousness and the blood of Christ." The *Bußkampf* the Moravians had once insisted on was now given up. "I saw," said David,

> that what I had hitherto so constantly insisted on—the *doing* so much and *feeling* so much, the long repentance and preparation for believing, the bitter sorrow for sin, and that deep contrition of heart which is found in some—were by no means essential to justification. We might be converted without prior repentance.

"Yea," David said later "that wherever the free grace of God is rightly preached, a sinner in the full career of his sins will probably receive, and be justified by it, before one who insists on such previous preparation." David dated the revolution to 1735. It "is now three years since, we have all chiefly insisted on *Christ given for us:* this we urge as the principal thing." Wesley disputed the date, however, "I dare not say this is right," he added in a footnote. From his own experience, he knew that long after 1735 *Bußkampf* piety had persisted among the Moravians in Georgia.[52]

What Wesley learned in Herrnhut made no difference to what he taught in England. The first sermon he preached on returning from Germany was not on blood and wounds but repentance and the remission of sins. Self-condemnation was deliberately encouraged. On 17 September 1739, at Plaistow, Wesley preached on "Blessed are those that mourn," saying: "It pleased God to give us in that hour two living instances of that piercing sense both of the guilt and power of sin, that dread of the wrath of God, and that full conviction of man's inability either to remove the power, or atone for the guilt, of sin (called by the world, despair)." This was *Bußkampf* piety. Poverty of spirit and mourning are spoken of as the "gate of Christian blessedness."[53] His brother, Charles, thought it unproductive to tell converts of their salvation before the time was ripe: "It is good for the choicest of God's children to receive (and that for a long time) the sentence of death in themselves." Referring to a penitent whom "he had convinced of sin," Charles wrote, "I have hardly known a soul under stronger convictions. Her expressions are full of self-abhorrence." In his diary, John Wesley made note of penitents who were convinced and mourners who were comforted.[54] Manifestations of despair were encouraged. It was these manifestations that alarmed Philip Molther when he first saw Wesley's penitents at Fetter Lane:

> The good people, not knowing rightly what they wanted, had adopted many most extraordinary ways. The very first time I entered their meeting, I was alarmed and almost terror-stricken at hearing their sighing and groaning, which strange proceedings they called the demonstration of the Spirit and of power.[55]

The moment Molther turned up, trouble could not be avoided. Wesley had told people to repent. Committed to the *Versöhnungslehre*, Molther told them to rejoice. The two agreed in thinking it was faith that saved; they did not agree on understanding how that faith was to be sought. In short, they could not preach from the same pulpit.

With or without Molther, the Fetter Lane schism was an event waiting to happen. Throughout the Moravian connection, the *Versöhnungslehre* was being propagated. Wesley was not alone. Inevitably, people drilled in the *Bußkampf* would resist. In Jena, the leader of the local society protested against excessive dictation by the Moravians, and the Moravians complained about his reluctance to promote "blood and wounds." Before coming to England, Molther had been stationed in Jena and probably found nothing new in the opposition he met at Fetter Lane. In the Ebersdorf society the introduction of the *Versöhnungslehre* provoked a long civil war that ended only in 1749 when the dissidents were expelled.[56] Winners often take their success for granted and fail to commemorate the losers. In the Moravian record, the resistance to the *Versöhnungslehre* is not easy to reconstruct; but resistance did occur, and the Fetter Lane schism was not unique. No doubt, in most cases, the dissidents left one at a time and found refuge in other Pietist societies. The Fetter Lane schism was a noisier, more turbulent event, one that was larger in its consequences. Hence more is known about it. What is known, however, comes from the Methodist, not the Moravian, side of the dispute. Little reference is made to Wesley in Moravian documents. In Georg Loskiel's history of the Moravian mission in America, it is mentioned that the brethren met Benjamin Ingham in Georgia. Ingham had gone to Georgia with Wesley and later joined the Moravians. No reference is made to Wesley.[57] Moravians are more important in the history of Methodism than are Methodists in the history of Moravianism.

When Zinzendorf condemned the *Bußkampf,* the opponents he primarily thought about were not the Methodists in England but the Pietists in Germany, particularly Pietists associated with Halle: "fools who dream up systems to run their own lives, and think, if it works for them, it must work for you."[58] With respect to the *Bußkampf,* however, Pietism and Methodism were identical. "The Pietist or the Methodist . . . catches sight of his misery and makes it an object of constant study. Happily . . . we see the wounds . . . of Christ and are comforted."[59] The *Bußkampf* implied that belief was something the convert might effect in himself. It was not a free gift he received without merit, but something he might earn by penance. Belief is turned into a kind of good work. This was Francke's great mistake. "We are damned by unbelief," said Zinzendorf; "but our belief will not save us if it is claimed . . . to be a work."[60] Methodists and Pietists replied, charging Zinzendorf with antinomianism. Faith was exalted at the expense of the law. Before belief, no repentance was required; after belief was attained, no real sanctity could be hoped for. In theory at least, this minimized the obligations of the law. The Moravians were, on Wesley's account, "the most plausible, and therefore far the most dangerous of all the Antinomians now in England." In *Farther Thoughts upon Christian Perfection* (1763), Moravianism becomes "the most refined antinomianism that ever was under the sun." It encouraged "the grossest libertinism, and most flagrant breach of every moral precept, such as could only have sprung from the abuse of true Christian experience."[61] Here, Wesley does not revert to some kind of high-Anglican asceticism. In Pietist circles in Germany, the charge of antinomianism was commonplace. Sigmund Baumgarten, a theologian in Halle, would not say that Moravians shared all the delusions of the old *Gesetzstürmer,* yet what they preached favored the revival of antinomianism. Like Wesley, he thought that the *Versöhnungslehre* hindered the convert's progress in attaining faith. Antinomianism is stressed by Joachim Lange and Johann Walch in their attacks on the Moravians. Walch was professor of philosophy at Jena, and Lange professor of theology at Halle; both were Pietists.[62]

What identifies Moravianism is the priority of "blood and wounds" with Methodism, it is the conviction of sin. In 1743, Wesley published the *General Rules of the United Societies,* in which the first Methodists are identified as people who approached him in London in 1739, "deeply convinced of sin, and earnestly groaning for redemption." No doubt, these are the same people whom Molther saw at Fetter Lane, "sighing and groaning." Wesley was asked to direct them "and advise them how to flee from the wrath to come; which they saw continually hanging over their heads." Wesley agreed to meet them regularly. "This was the rise of the United Society, first in London, and then in other places." Like early Herrnhut, the Society set itself up as a *Bußkampf* association.

> Such a society is no other than "a company of men having the form and seeking the power of godliness, united in order to pray together, to receive the word of exhortation, and to watch over one another in love, that they may help each other to work out their salvation."

Small classes were instituted for the members "that it may the more easily be discerned, whether they are indeed working out their own salvation."[63] Conviction of sin became the minimum test for admission. "There is only one condition previously required in those who desire admission," states the *General Rules,* "—a desire 'to flee from the wrath to come, to be saved from their sins'." Both the Methodist and the Moravian thought of conversion as a psychological crisis. For the Moravian, it is precipitated by the knowledge of salvation, for the Methodist by the knowledge of guilt. The Methodist will not be saved until he learns what the Moravian knows. The Methodist, however, is expected to get these things in their proper order: first guilt, then redemption. Knowledge of redemption never supersedes knowledge of guilt as a condition of membership. Those who remain in the society must continue to "evidence their desire of salvation." He who does not ceases to be a member. "We will admonish him of the error of his ways," Wesley wrote; "we will bear with him for a season: But then if he repent not, he hath no place among us."[64]

That conviction comes before faith was something Wesley continued to insist upon. In a sense, it is the distress of the *Bußkampf* that identifies Methodism in the public mind. Methodists are thought of as people whose faith is testified to in enthusiastic demonstrations. As evidence of conviction, demonstrations were, in fact, countenanced by Wesley. Wesley describes the case of a woman in 1739 who was seized "with little less than the agonies of death." Wesley prayed "that God who had brought her to the birth, would give her the strength to bring forth." Over five days, "she travailed and groaned, being in bondage." Then *Durchbruch* or break-through was attained. "On Thursday evening our Lord got Himself the victory; and from that moment she has been full of love and joy." The sufferings the convert felt in the travail of the *Bußkampf* might be caused by evil spirits, evil spirits who torment sinners struggling to escape from sin. The sufferings could also be explained without any supernatural supposition.

> For how easy it is to suppose that a strong, lively, and sudden apprehension of the heinousness of sin, the wrath of God, and the bitter pains of eternal death, should affect the body as well as the soul. . . . Yea, we may question whether . . . it be possible for the mind to be affected in so violent a degree without some or other of those bodily symptoms following.

Even symptoms of madness might naturally be expected from those who labor under conviction. "It is not strange . . . that some should fancy they see the flames of hell, or the devil and his angels around them." The symptoms of course were temporary.

> All these, and whatever less common effects may sometimes accompany this conviction, are easily known from the natural distemper of madness, were it only by this one circumstance, —that whenever the person convinced tastes the pardoning love of God, they all vanish away in a moment.[65]

Wesley did not regard these signs as infallible proof that conviction was taking place. "I speak of them," he said, "as 'outward symptoms which have often accompanied the inward work of God.' Often, I say, not always, not necessarily: they may, or they may not. This work may be without those symptoms, and those symptoms may be without this work." Their frequency diminished. "They sometimes occur still, but not often," Wesley wrote in 1768. Nor was it a matter of importance. "And we do not regard whether they occur or not, knowing that the essence of religion, righteousness, peace, and joy in the Holy Ghost, is quite independent upon them."[66] Perhaps Methodists lost interest in fits and convulsions. This does not mean, however, that they came to deny the need for the *Bußkampf* as a preliminary to faith. The Pietism the Moravians had taught him in Savannah persisted. "Many have, and many do daily experience an unspeakable change," Wesley wrote in 1761. "After being deeply convinced of inbred sin, particularly of pride, anger, self-will, and unbelief, in a moment they feel all faith and love."[67] In a sermon entitled "The Way to the Kingdom," Wesley preached on Mark 1:15: "The kingdom of God is at hand: Repent ye, and believe the gospel." Again, the priority of repentance is asserted. "First, repent, that is, know yourselves." Then follow the usual *Bußkampf* prescriptions: "Know thyself to be a sinner. . . . Know that corruption of thy inmost nature. . . . Know that thou art corrupted in every power, in every faculty. . . . So that there is no soundness in thy soul . . . there are only 'wounds and bruises, and putrefying sores.'" The sinner must acknowledge his unbelief, his viciousness. "Who can number the sands of the sea, or the drops of rain, or thy iniquities?" The sinner must recognize that he deserves damnation. "Thou art guilty of everlasting death. It is the just reward of thy inward and outward wickedness. It is just that the sentence should now take place. Dost thou see, dost thou feel this? Art thou thoroughly convinced that thou deservest God's wrath, and everlasting damnation?" Then he must recognize his utter helplessness. "Begin now: Make the trial. Shake off that outward sin that so easily besetteth thee. Thou canst not. . . . for, so long as the tree remains evil, it cannot bring forth good fruit." The sinner is dead and cannot inspire himself with life. "Thou art utterly without strength." All he may do is feel sorrow, and repent. "If to this lively conviction of thy . . . sins . . . there be added suitable affections, —sorrow of heart, . . . remorse, and self-condemnation, . . . shame to lift up thy eyes to heaven, —fear of the wrath of God abiding on thee," then belief may be attained. "I say unto thee, in the name of the Lord, 'Thou art not far from the kingdom of God.' One step more and thou shalt enter in. Thou dost 'repent.' Now, 'believe the gospel.'"[68] In the sermon, "The Spirit of Bondage and of Adoption," the penitent figures as a captive struggling vainly against the power of sin. "He truly desires to break loose from sin, and begins to struggle with it. . . . The more he strives, wishes, labours to be free, the more does he feel his chains. . . . He is still in

bondage and fear. . . . Thus he toils without end, repenting and sinning, and repenting and sinning."[69]

Both "The Spirit of Bondage" and "The Way to the Kingdom"
counted among the standard sermons that Methodist preachers must
subscribe to if they were to preach in Methodist chapels. Wesley
never changed his mind about the priority of repentance. The point
he defended against the Moravians in the Fetter Lane schism, he
continued to insist on to the end. Where he did change his mind,
however, is in the degree of hope that is conceded to the penitent
struggling in the *Bußkampf*. When the sermons were written, the
penitent was regarded as a child of the Devil. Indeed, the purpose
of the *Bußkampf* is to convince the penitent of this truth. He could
not, in any sense, claim to be in the favor of God. "We have always
taught," Wesley wrote, "that a penitent mourned or was pained on
this very account, because he felt he was 'not in the favour of God,'
having a sense of guilt upon his conscience and a sense of the divine
displeasure at the same time." As late as 1768, Wesley thought this
was what Methodists should teach. Anything else

> tends to lull mourners to sleep; to make them cry, "Peace, peace," to
> their souls, "when there is no peace." It directly tends to damp and still
> their convictions, and encourage them to sit down contented before
> Christ is revealed to them and before the Spirit witnesses with their spirits
> that they are children of God.[70]

Before his death, however, Wesley relented. The child of the Devil is
promoted to servant of God. In his very despair, the penitent may
discern a mark of divine encouragement. He is given grounds for
hope that he may persist and will receive saving faith. "'He that
believeth,' as a child of God, 'hath the witness in himself.' This the
servant hath not. Yet let no man discourage him; rather lovingly
exhort him to expect it every moment."[71] Having argued that saving
faith commences in the conviction of sin, Wesley could not deny
that conviction of sin is a good thing, that it manifests some kind of
grace from which the penitent could derive hope.

From the very beginning, Wesley was committed to a conception
of conversion that presupposed stages. The faith of the servant represents the addition of a new degree, not a radical change in soteriol-
ogy. The servant of God still lacks faith. As a child of the Devil on
the old *Bußkampf* scale, he received that faith in his despair. On the

new *Bußkampf* scale, he despaired and in his despair saw grounds
for hope:

> Exhort him to press on, by all possible means, till he passes 'from faith
> to faith'; from the faith of a *servant* to the faith of a *son;* from the spirit
> of bondage unto fear, to the spirit of childlike love: He will then have
> 'Christ revealed in his heart.'[72]

In discerning a new stage in the *Bußkampf,* however, the point he
had insisted on in the Fetter Lane schism is not abandoned. Penance
comes before faith, and conversion is something that proceeds in
degrees.

3

Connexion

THE METHODIST REVIVAL COINCIDED WITH THE EVANGELICAL REVIVAL IN THE Church of England. The two revivals were not dissimilar; in some respects, their membership even overlapped. George Whitefield, the Countess of Huntingdon, William Grimshaw, and John Fletcher can be fairly counted as important figures in the history of either movement. What Methodists and Evangelicals had in common was their conception of conversion. For both, conversion entailed a psychological crisis. Whitefield's conversion was not unlike Wesley's; it began with a conviction of sin. "My comforts were soon withdrawn, and a horrible fearfulness and dread permitted to overwhelm my soul." After conviction came faith. "God was pleased to remove the heavy load to enable me to lay hold of His dear Son by a living faith, and by giving me the Spirit of adoption to seal me even to the day of everlasting redemption."[1] For James Hervey, another Evangelical, conviction was "the preparative" for the reception of faith. The penitent had to cultivate within himself a sense of his "great depravity," his "extreme guilt" and his "utterly undone condition."[2] In theology, the Evangelical revival was Calvinist; the Methodist revival was not. This difference sometimes brought the two into conflict. No less important, however, were their differences in ecclesiology and their inability to agree on how the revival ought to be directed. Evangelicals were churchmen and in the main worked within the parish. People were to be converted where they worshipped. Evangelicals aimed at putting in every parish a "godly minister." Funds were collected to help in the education of Evangelical students at Oxford and Cambridge. In Cambridge, Charles Simeon founded the Simeon Trust to buy up church patronage for the appointment of Evangelicals at the parish level.[3] Methodists worked outside the church. Wesley did not concern himself with the appointment of godly ministers, nor does anything in Methodism correspond to the Simeon Trust.

The Methodist revival worked through the Connexion, an association of local societies set up independently of the church and its jurisdictional divisions. What we know about the structure of this connexion comes largely from Wesley himself, often from statements in which he explains how the connexion should run. What should happen and what does happen are different things. It is tempting to suppose greater uniformity and regularity than perhaps in fact existed. The basic unit in the Connexion was the local society. Local societies must have varied enormously in size. No rules existed concerning maximum and minimum membership, and we do not know how large or small the societies actually were. Anyone who wished to flee the wrath to come, or to be saved from sin, could be admitted. In its original intention, the qualification supposed that the candidate had been awakened and was laboring under conviction. There was no credal or denominational test. The candidate did not even have to profess Christianity. Formal control of membership was supplied by a "ticket" that was renewed every quarter and which allowed the holder to attend society meetings. Who got the ticket, and who did not, was decided by Wesley or by a preacher acting on his behalf. The member who failed to have his ticket reissued was, in effect, expelled from the society.[4] Expulsion from the society, however, did not mean excommunication from a church. The right to expel was a secular authority, not an ecclesiastical one. "I did not exert it as a priest," Wesley wrote, "but as one whom that Society had voluntarily chosen to be at the head of them." It was the authority "any steward of a Society exerts by the consent of the other members. I did neither more nor less than declare that they who had broken our rules were no longer of our Society."[5]

Each local society was divided into smaller units where members met under the direction of their own leaders. These units were of two kinds. In the first, membership was decided by spiritual progress. Those who had saving faith went to the *bands,* those who sought sanctification to *select societies.* Those who had fallen from faith, or who had not yet attained it, went to the *penitents.* Here, the principle of division is pietistic and corresponds to what we find in early Moravianism. The second kind of unit was the class. Not pietistic in its principle of division, this unit corresponds to the type of unit that emerged in later Moravianism. In the class, the membership is unsegregated; the sanctified, the justified and the penitent all met together. Initially class members were visited in their homes by the class leader and the members were selected on the basis of where they lived.[6] In principle, the Methodist class corresponds to what came to be called "the choir" in Moravianism. The class and the choir are devotional subdivisions, and in both, members were selected without reference to their spiritual progress. In the choirs, members were chosen according to their status: infants, children, young men, young women, married men, married women, widows, widowers. No attention was paid to the member's place of residence. In a large society like Herrnhut or Herrnhaag or Bethlehem, Moravians lived together on the same estate, where locality was useless as a basis of selection. Had Wesley been a wealthy landlord presiding over his private Herrnhut, Methodism might well have instituted choirs on the Moravian pattern. In setting up their small groups, Moravians and Methodists alike used a double system of classification, one spiritual in its standard of selection, the other nonspiritual. The spiritual system disappeared in Moravianism with the adoption of the *Versöhnungslehre*. Had Wesley followed the Moravians, the bands, the select societies and the penitential groups would have disappeared in Methodism as well. Their survival presupposes that the convert in the reception of faith progresses through stages. Methodism retained what Moravianism abandoned. In the administration of Methodism, however, the unsegregated class proved more important than the segregated bands. Dues were paid weekly at the class meeting; and every quarter, membership tickets were renewed.[7] Over time, the class took on functions which perhaps properly belonged to the bands and select societies. Class lists surviving from the eighteenth century show individual members identified according to their spiritual progress. The leader who did his job was expected to guide the members of the class in their spiritual progress from one level to the next.[8] The segregated groups disappeared during the nineteenth century.

Within each local society a committee of stewards was appointed. This was done by Wesley or by lay preachers acting on his behalf. Wesley resisted efforts to have the stewards appointed by the society. "We have not, and never had, any such custom. We are no republicans, and never intend to be." The chairmanship of the committee rotated. The stewards received and disbursed Society funds. Whatever discretion the stewards possessed was exercised under the supervision of Wesley or the preacher he appointed. In a version of the rules issued in 1747, the stewards might do nothing "without the

consent of the Minister, either actually had, or reasonably presumed."[9] Where a local society erected a meetinghouse, title to the
property was vested in the trustees. The first trustees were appointed
in Bristol in 1739. The Bristol settlement predates the break with the
Moravians. Trustees may or may not have been the same people who
acted as stewards. As trustees, however, they were the legal owners
of the property they administered and, unlike the stewards, could
not be dictated to or removed at will. Wesley's authority was pre-
served by adoption of the "model deed" which came to be the standard form under which trustees were appointed. In this, Wesley is
named as the beneficiary for whom the trust was held. The trustees
might, in law, own the property, but, in equity, it is held for Wesley's
use. Only Wesley or someone he appointed could preach in the
meetinghouse. This power of appointment was the real basis of Wesley's authority. A simple property right, its exercise by him assumed
no spiritual or ecclesiastical status. Had Wesley died before 1784,
the right to appoint would have passed to whomever his heir at law
happened to be. In 1784, he bequeathed it by deed poll to the Methodist annual conference. The transfer did not take effect until his
death. The bequest is sometimes thought of as the event marking
the foundation of a corporate Methodist church. More accurately, it
is a real estate transaction that transfers a property right from one
owner to another. Its ecclesiastical significance is negligible.[10]

Within the Connexion, local societies were not directly related to
each other. What joined them was their common relationship with
Wesley. It was with him, and not with each other, that the connexion
existed.[11] On Wesley's understanding, the relationship derived essentially from contract or agreement. It had started when the first penitents sought his direction. "Here commenced my power; namely, a
power to appoint when, and where and how they should meet; and
to remove those whose lives showed that they had not a desire
'to flee from the wrath to come.'" The expansion of Methodism in
membership made no difference. "And this power remained the
same, whether the people meeting together were twelve, or twelve
hundred, or twelve thousand." The relationship was founded on consent alone. "Every member may leave me when he pleases. But while
he chooses to stay, it is on the same terms that he joined me at
first."[12] In his relationship to Methodist membership, Wesley is more
like Hobbes's Leviathan than Filmer's Patriarch. With the expansion
of Methodism, he turned to the use of lay preachers. The preacher

indirectly provided the spiritual direction Wesley himself could not provide. Societies were grouped into "circuits," and within each circuit a preacher looked after several societies which paid his salary. At regular intervals, the preacher was reassigned to a new circuit. Itinerancy made it difficult for the preacher to put down roots in a specific society, to establish a personal following and, in effect, usurp Wesley's authority. The preachers were laymen, not priests; they might preach or give spiritual guidance, but they were forbidden to administer the sacraments or direct public worship. Wesley's authority over them was, in no sense, episcopal or apostolic. In its defense, he again appealed to contract. The preachers had freely chosen to help him in his work and on his terms. "Observe: These . . . desired me, not I them." Here commenced his power,

> to appoint each of these when and where and how to labor; that is, while he chose to continue with me. For each had a power to go away when he pleased; as I had also to go away from them, or any of them, if I saw sufficient cause.

The expansion of Methodism made no difference. "On these terms, and no other we joined at first," Wesley said; "on these we continued joined." Once a year, Wesley met the preachers in conference. Here, they were assigned to their new circuits and consulted on points of government and doctrine. The function of the conference was in no sense legislative. Referring to its members, Wesley wrote, "Observe: I myself sent for these of my own free choice. And I sent for them to advise, not govern me. Neither did I at any time divest myself of any part of the power . . . which the providence of God had cast upon me."[13] Consultation did not mean submission. Until Wesley dies and the conference inherits his property rights under the deed poll, it will not emerge as the governing body within the Connexion.

Historians often suppose that the Methodist Connexion was something that developed in its constitution through trial and error. Frank Baker denies the influence of any prior plan. The societies were founded as "expedients forced upon a man ready to utilize almost any methods to accomplish what he regarded as a divine mission." The expedient Wesley selected "might be derived from ecclesiastical practice ancient or modern, from church or sect; it might equally well come from the committee room or the law court, from Parliament or prayer meeting. It might be the result of 'pure chance'." Henry Rack agrees with Baker. According to Rack, the Connexion emerges "piecemeal in response to circumstances." In its developed form, the structure was "strikingly different from that of most other eighteenth-century churches and religious associations." Its development was unplanned; it emerged "through a series of accidents and improvisations." Wesley "always maintained that this was so and he was right. The various institutions were developed by a process of trial and error, borrowing and adaptation, occasionally outright invention."[14] Here, scholarship follows Wesley's own version of the facts—first stated by him in 1748 in a private letter to one of his clerical allies, Vincent Perronet, and later published as the *Plain Account of the People called Methodists*. Wesley tells us that the Methodists "had not the least expectation at first of anything like what has since followed." There was "no previous design or plan at all." "Just as the occasion offered," the Connexion took shape. Methodists

> saw or felt some impending or pressing evil or some good end necessary to be pursued. And many times they fell unawares on the very thing which secured the good or removed the evil. At other times they consulted on the most probable means following only common sense and Scripture.[15]

Like Wesley's other historical recollections, *Plain Account* says nothing about the Moravians or the society at Fetter Lane. The formation of the Moorfields society is accounted for as the direct response to the need of awakened sinners. The sinners are not named, nor is it explained how Wesley first came to meet them. They simply rose up out of the ground. "One and another and another came to us, asking what they should do, being distressed on every side," and Wesley urged them: "'Strengthen you one another. Talk together as often as you can. And pray earnestly with and for one another, that you may "endure to the end and be saved.'" In giving this advice, Wesley was prompted only by reason and Scripture. On further solicitation, Wesley met the penitents singly in their private houses. Then, for reasons of convenience, he proposed meeting them together every Thursday evening and directing them in their conversion. Thus, on Wesley's account, arose the first Methodist society, "without any previous design on either side." The innovation of the classes was credited to the suggestion of a member in Bristol. Their first purpose was to raise money. The leader of each class undertook to visit its members once a week and collect donations. In time, it was discovered that the class visit provided the Society with a way to look after its members in their spiritual and moral welfare. "It struck me immediately," wrote Wesley, "'This is the thing; the very thing we have wanted so long.'" The class leader was encouraged to make "a particular inquiry into the behavior of those whom he saw weekly." For reasons of convenience, the household visits became weekly meetings. At these meetings, members confessed their faults to one another and sought counsel. "Advice or reproof was given as need required, quarrels made up, misunderstandings removed; and after an hour or two was spent in this labor of love; they concluded with prayer and thanksgiving." At the solicitation of the converted members, the bands were set up. These, wrote Wesley, "wanted some means of closer union. . . . In compliance with their desire, I divided them into smaller companies." Those who lapsed from saving faith needed special treatment, hence the institution of separate meetings for penitents: "The exhortations and prayers used among the believers did no longer profit these. They wanted advice and instruction suited to their case; which as soon as I observed, I separated them from the rest, and desired them to meet me apart on Saturday evenings." Again, Wesley sees Methodism in its constitutional development responding to circumstances as they arise.[16] In the *Plain Account*, little is said about lay preachers. Here, the reader is referred to explanations Wesley had published earlier in his *Farther Appeal to Men of Reason and Religion* (1745). Like everything else in Methodism, the appointment of lay preachers is understood as an unforeseen reaction to necessity. God provided what was required.

> "Out of the stones he raised up" those who should beget "children to Abraham." We had no more foresight of this than you: Nay, we had the deepest prejudices against it; until we could not but own that God gave "wisdom from above" to these unlearned and ignorant men, so that the work of the Lord prospered in their hand, and sinners were daily converted to God.[17]

Whatever is owed the Moravians, Wesley does not acknowledge. In this, his statement of what happened is massively uncandid.

The Moravian brotherhood, on its broadest definition, divides into two different memberships—that of the congregation brethren and that of the diaspora brethren. What distinguishes the two types is the ecclesiastical status of the local assemblies in which the members met. The *congregation* brethren formed regular congregations, or *Gemeine*, in which their own clergy might direct public worship. The diaspora brethren met in societies that did not function as churches; for public worship and holy communion, *diaspora* brethren, like the Methodists, went elsewhere. Within Germany, it was the diaspora association that largely prevailed; outside Germany, and particularly in the colonies, it was the congregational association. To overstate things somewhat, outside Germany, Moravians tended to constitute a church, in Germany a society.[18] Insofar as they did not conduct public worship and attended the local Lutheran church, the Moravians who lived in Herrnhut belonged to the diaspora, not the congregation system. As we shall see, the same double identity manifests itself in Methodism. When Wesley ordained preachers to serve in America and Scotland, he implicitly sanctioned the forming of congregations that would function as churches. Within England, ordination was withheld; there, Methodism persisted as a society. For Zinzendorf and Wesley, the motives were possibly the same: Zinzendorf did not wish to challenge the Lutheran church in Germany, nor Wesley the Anglican church in England. Overseas, however, congregations could be sanctioned that were not, in a technical sense, schismatic. In the relationship between Methodism and Moravianism, the double identity of each is not important. What *is* important is the constitution of the diaspora network. It is from this network that the Methodist Connexion derives.

In its largest sense, *diaspora* refers to Christians who are real believers. They may belong to any denomination, but as members of the diaspora they find their unity in the invisible church of Christ. In a more special sense, the term refers to believers organized into local societies set up and tended by Moravian missionaries. What varied was the degree of association between the missionaries and the societies they served. The one constant was that diaspora members remained within their own churches and did not become Moravians for purposes of formal worship. As a word, *diaspora* is seldom used in Moravian records before 1750. Here, the institution antedates the word. Earlier diaspora brethren were sometimes referred to as step-brethren, cousins, external brethren, or brethren *nach dem Fleisch*. Local diaspora societies were sometimes referred to as associate societies or as Jesus-congregations. A list from the year 1742 testifies to the existence of almost 700 societies, 480 of them with precise addresses. Most were German, but some were found outside Germany: sixty-six in Switzerland; thirty-two in Holland; two in Sweden; six in Norway; four in Hungary; and twelve in France, Hesse, and England.[19] The mission started in the 1720s. It is significant that

Zinzendorf did not reconstitute the ordination of the ancient Moravian church until after the diaspora system had emerged. When he did reconstitute the church, its operation was restricted to the non-German world. Like Methodism, Moravianism is a layman's association that takes on the functions of a church. It is not a church that embarks on a mission to the laity. The first of the diaspora societies was founded in 1728 in Jena, where a revival movement at the university had begun. A formal society with its own bylaws was instituted. In structure and organization, the Jena society resembled the one at Herrnhut. Societies founded later tended to get their Moravian institutions introduced in installments. Despite its proximity to Herrnhut in structure, Jena was not subordinate to Herrnhut in any administrative sense; like Fetter Lane, Jena was autonomous. Its non-Moravian character was something Zinzendorf insisted on. "Herrnhut has its Moravians but not Jena. There it is a *jenaische* and not a Moravian brotherhood . . . that exists."[20] Whether Zinzendorf was right or wrong here, depends on what is meant by *Moravian*. Like Fetter Lane, Jena had been set up on the advice of the Moravians. It was Moravian in its institutions; it received Moravian missionaries. But, in its administration, it was independent.

The connection between Jena and the other diaspora societies was supplied by Moravian missionaries like Peter Böhler and Philip Molther. Initially, these advisers were called "messengers,"or *Boten,* and eventually workers, or *Arbeiter.* Sometimes, like Böhler and Molther, the workers were clergy who had been ordained in the reconstituted Moravian church; more often, they were not. Working as spiritual advisers in the direction of individual converts, ordination was superfluous to any purpose the missionaries served in the diaspora world. They were not there to conduct public worship. The Moravian diaspora resembles the Methodist Connexion in that the only constitutional relationship between the local societies in each association arose from the reception of a common ministry appointed from outside. Whether ordained or not, Moravians acknowledged a duty to call everyone to salvation. The special mission to the diaspora emerges from a background in Herrnhut, where people evangelized as the opportunity arose. In 1727, workers were for the first time sent out on specific assignment. The diaspora worker was the model from which the Methodist preacher was derived. Like the preacher, the diaspora worker was a layman, his appointment to the society temporary. He itinerates between a number of societies scattered over the district to which he has been assigned. Also like the preacher, the diaspora worker discouraged any society that wanted to turn itself into a separatist conventicle and conduct its own public worship.

The diaspora mission developed piecemeal over a period of years. There was no model for the Moravians to follow, and the system exhibited a greater diversity of form than the Methodist Connexion. The first workers we know of were active in the vicinity of Herrnhut. In 1728, they went farther afield, to Brandenburg, Sweden, Denmark, and England. Between September 1727 and April 1728, Christian David and Christian Demuth were active in Silesia. Because Silesia was still under Hapsburg government, what they were doing there was illegal. The conversion they preached was a Pietist one, a conversion that could be attained through penance. "There was nothing too much that they could say for the law, to awaken the soul" complained the Lutheran minister at Heidersdorf. This directly contradicted what diaspora workers would later teach.[21] It did not contradict what was taught in the Methodist mission. In 1738, two workers turned up at Lissa, in Poland, the site of an old Moravian congregation whose origins went back to the Hussite church in Bohemia. Like Wesley in England, the Moravian diaspora workers were encroaching on territory that technically belonged to their own denomination. Here, they tried to convert the Moravian pastor, Senior Sitkovius, to the new gospel of "blood and wounds," but to no avail. A diaspora society was set up, and the workers moved on. In the case of Fetter Lane, more than a year passed between the departure of Böhler and the arrival of Molther. In Lissa, it was three years; when the workers returned, the Society had fallen apart and had to be reestablished. Relations between the diaspora mission and the authentic Moravian church in Lissa were no less uncordial than those between the Methodist Connexion and the Church of England.[22] Zinzendorf spoke of the Lissa pastor as a "stiff-necked Calvinist." One of the workers said Sitkovius was too much of a rationalist to understand the Gospel they preached. For his part, Sitkovius thought no better of the workers, and threatened them with the law; members of his congregation who joined diaspora societies risked excommunication. The old Moravians in Lissa were no better than nominal Christians everywhere. They dressed respectably and claimed to be believers, complained one of the workers. "But this doesn't stop them from carousing in the taverns, and gambling and cursing. Those who don't spend their time drinking are the exception."[23]

Württemberg possibly is the first place where we find an organized circuit with several societies assigned to the care of a permanent worker. In 1739, Johann Lange was sent to the Stuttgart area, where a start had been made for him to build on. Zinzendorf had worked in the area four years earlier, and "awakened souls" had been identified. Lange organized them into formal societies with their own rules. What Peter Böhler did on a small scale at Fetter Lane, Lange did on a larger scale in Württemberg. The difference is that Lange remained in Württemberg and continued to work with the societies that had been set up on his advice. As a rule, each circuit had its own diaspora worker. Lange was assigned to three and was responsible for an area that lay within a thirty-mile radius of Stuttgart.[24] He received no salary and had to earn his living as an itinerant tailor. Close supervision of the societies was difficult, since each society was visited, at most, once or twice a year. Societies were expected to run themselves. In setting them up, attention was paid to the kind of spiritual leadership and direction they would receive from their own members. In Lomersheim, in the Enz circuit, seven elders were appointed: three men, two women, and two unmarried young people who were brother and sister. Lange reported back to Zinzendorf that one of the men was the village schoolmaster. A week earlier, this man had found grace and come to trust entirely in the blood of Jesus. The brother and sister were particularly well suited for the guidance of others, Lange informed Zinzendorf. The woman was a witness to the truth and a great fighter. The man was powerful in testimony and responded to the needs of those he counseled with a solicitude that was "sehr mütterlich" (that is, very motherly).[25] The elder here is not unlike a Methodist class leader, in that both play a part in the spiritual direction of others. Württemberg is exceptional in its decentralization. In the neighborhood of large Moravian settlements like Herrnhut and Herrnhaag, diaspora workers could be recruited in greater numbers. Here, too, visits were more frequent and control more closely exercised.[26]

In setting up diaspora societies, Moravians proceeded with caution. They did not preach in the open air. The parson was often consulted before a society was set up in his parish. In the mission to the Estonians and Latvians in the Baltic territories, the Moravians for a time worked in collaboration with the Lutheran clergy. The object of the diaspora mission was to arouse people to the realities of Christian faith, not to disturb them in their allegiance to their own denominations or to convert them to the Moravian church. How well the Moravians got on with the parish clergy was something they liked to emphasize in their public statements. David Cranz writes of Lutherans and Moravians doing God's work in a spirit of "fellowship" and "accord." Every *Gemeine* had a friendly parson in the neighborhood with whom "it was settled how awakened souls might best be taken care of."[27] Like the Methodists in England, the Moravians often were hated, particularly by the parish clergy. Nevertheless, friendly clergy did exist who worked with the Moravians in the diaspora mission. In 1754, Zinzendorf convened a small number of these in the first diaspora conference. This became an annual event with an average attendance of fifty to sixty ministers.[28] The first of the parish clergy to work the diaspora mission came from the neighborhood of Herrnhut, in Saxony. In 1732, Pastor Manitius, the minister in Hauswalde, attached himself to the mission, and in 1734 Pastor Schneider, the minister in Neukirch. Because of their diaspora work, both Schnieder and Manitius got in trouble with the local authorities. The Neukirch society numbered nearly a hundred. In 1737, Schneider was forced to sign a statement promising to stop holding conventicles. Karl Rudolf Reichel followed Schnieder as pastor in Neukirch and carried on the mission. He was appointed in 1754, and under his direction the society's membership tripled. Reichel held devotional meetings in his own house. From time to time, he was helped by a diaspora worker appointed by the Moravians. Four times a year, the members of the Neukirch society received communion together. Not surprisingly, this was a Lutheran service, not a Moravian one, and was administered by Reichel as the Lutheran incumbent. Once a year, the pre-communion *Sprechen* was conducted by a diaspora worker sent to Neukirch for that purpose. At other times, presumably, the *Sprechen* was conducted by Reichel or one of the lay members in the society. In Bayreuth, the diaspora mission was directed by Johann Steinmetz, the Lutheran pastor and superintendent at Neustadt. In 1731, the Moravians numbered their adherents in Neustadt at seventy-five: twenty-six brothers and thirty-six sisters in the town itself, and thirteen brothers in neighboring villages.[29] The Moravians maintained similar contacts with Reformed congregations. Herrnhaag had been founded for this specific purpose. Less is known about the Calvinist than the Lutheran diaspora, although a Calvinist diaspora certainly existed. Cranz refers to a network ranging from Westphalia and the Palatinate to Switzerland and France. In Basel, one of town clergy, Pfarrer Ryhiner, directed the meetings of the Society in the 1740s. Ryhiner eventually broke with the Moravians. Although not without some troubled periods, the Basel society managed to preserve good relations with the Reformed church, and a few of its members were recruited from the parish clergy and candidates for ordination.[30] Members joined on the understanding that they would continue to attend the church they already belonged to. In England, candidates were expected to sign a standard form in which they denied that they wished to leave the church: "Much more, we wish to remain within it and conduct ourselves as its worthy members." For instance, a member who left the church in 1743 was expelled from a diaspora society in London.[31] A Methodist might be expelled for the same reason. In Methodism, this reflects Wesley's background in the Moravian diaspora as much as it does a special fidelity to the Church of England. Neither in the diaspora nor in the Methodist Connexion, was it his purpose to set up a new denomination.

There was no prescribed constitution that the diaspora societies had to adopt. Those set up on the pattern of Herrnhut or Herrnhaag possessed a large number of officers appointed for special functions: elders, helpers, and the president for temporal business; overseers, teachers, and band-leaders for religious education; and attendants, almoners, and visitors of the sick for charitable purposes. Such societies might also observe such Moravian ceremonies as footwashing, watchnight services, and love feasts.[32] The Jena society modeled itself on this pattern, which, in later foundations, was discouraged. Zinzendorf condemned what he called *Aftergemeine,* or mock congregations, where the rites and institutions of Herrnhut were mindlessly imitated. It was the spirit, not the practice, of Herrnhut that mattered. Diaspora brethren were not to cultivate distinctiveness and take on a denominational identity. In 1743, the society in Augsburg was disowned for persisting in the observance of Moravian ritual.[33] The full Herrnhut constitution, with all its officers and special assemblies, could work only in a society with a large membership. It was inappropriate for a small society that aspired to be nothing more than an intimate brotherhood. Herrnhut, moreover, was a unit of local government within Saxony. The constitution provided for numerous functions of local government, such as road repair, tax collection, and the administration of petty justice. None of this was needed at Fetter Lane.[34] Diaspora societies approximated the simplicity of Fetter Lane in their organization, not the complexity of Herrnhut. The one thing they possessed in common, however, was the subdivision of their membership into intimate, devotional groups where members might encourage each other in their spiritual progress. Admission into the band was one of Moravianism's strongest selling points in Germany. At Fetter Lane in 1738, formation of the bands ranked as the second item in the rules of the society. Members were to be "divided into several *bands,* or little companies," none "of fewer than five or more than ten persons." Each member was to speak in order, "as freely, plainly, and concisely as he can, the real state of his heart, with his several temptations and deliverances, since the last time of meeting." The bands were constituted on the old pattern with a segregated membership. After Wesley left Fetter Lane, they were suspended, and new groups were set up with an unsegregated membership.[35] These were called classes. The change may have been precipitated by the quarrel with Wesley, but more likely it came about as a direct result of the *Versöhnungslehre.* "The society . . . is not now in bands, as before," explained a brother at Fetter Lane. The bands no longer enjoyed "that blessing they used to have"; and members "did not know for what, or how they should use them." At the same time, the segregated band disappeared in the diaspora on the continent.[36] Only in Methodism did it persist.

Wesley's involvement with the diaspora began in Georgia. The Moravians who traveled with Wesley set up a society on arriving at Savannah. Bands were instituted. Given the intimacy of his relationship with the Moravians, it is fair to assume that Wesley was admitted as a member of one of the bands. In his journal for April 1736, Savannah is referred to as a "blessed place" where a kind of brotherhood exists that is consistent with band membership, "where, having but one end in view, dissembling and fraud are not; but each of us can pour out his heart without fear into his brother's bosom!" Another society was set up for the benefit of Wesley's parishioners. "And we agreed . . . to advise the more serious among them to form themselves into a sort of little society, and to meet once or twice a week, in order to reprove, instruct, and exhort one another." In the institution of these bands, the Moravian influence is unmistakable. Out of the membership, a small number were selected for more intimate union with each other, which might be forwarded, partly by our conversing singly with each, and partly by inviting them altogether to our house; and this, accordingly, we determined to do every Sunday in the afternoon.

In Germany, Moravians might help the minister direct the spiritual progress of society members; we cannot tell whether this happened in Savannah. Two months later, Wesley set up another society at Frederica. "We began to execute at Frederica what we had before agreed to do at Savannah." The Frederica society met Sunday in the afternoon. Wesley met the "most serious of the communicants" again in the evening after public service to spend time with them "in singing, reading, and conversation." Meetings were held also on weekdays. In collaborating with the Moravians in Georgia, Wesley took a position not unlike that of Lutheran and Reformed ministers in Germany. As the legal minister, he directed societies set up on the Moravian pattern. It is not impossible that the Moravians helped him manage the societies. The connection between the Moravians and Wesley had nothing to do with their respective church membership. In 1736, Moravian missionaries were not necessarily members of the Moravian church. Some were, however, but some belonged to the Reformed church, most, probably to the Lutheran. Back in Germany, those who belonged to the Moravian church suspended their membership and worshipped as Reformed or as Lutherans. On the evidence of Wesley's journal, there is no reason to think that the Moravians conducted separate public services in Savannah. To do so would have challenged his status as parish minister. It also would have departed from the Moravian's normal diaspora practice. It is fair to assume that, with everyone else, they attended the Sunday service that Wesley conducted.[37]

Upon his return to England, Wesley's involvement with the Moravians deepened. Those he met, along with Peter Böhler, on 7 February 1738, "a day much to be remembered," were bound for Georgia. In England, however, they did what they could to form societies. On 10 March, two months before Fetter Lane was founded, Wenzel Neißer reported the formation of a new society in London. "We have set up bands and every Sunday and Wednesday, hold a general meeting." On 18 April, Peter Böhler wrote from London, perhaps with reference to Neißer's society, perhaps to another, but certainly not to Fetter Lane, which was yet to be formed:

Last Sunday we held a love feast with ten youths and four grown men. We formed them into bands. Bands meet three times a week: Monday, Wednesday, and Friday. Those who are to direct the band meetings are chosen by lot.

On 17 February, Wesley accompanied Böhler on a mission to Oxford. In Stanton Harcourt, he introduced Böhler to his old friend from the days of the Holy Club, John Gambold. In Oxford itself, the Holy Club had vanished. Wesley introduced Böhler to its one survivor, John Sarney, "the only one now remaining here of the many who . . . were used to 'take sweet counsel together,' and rejoice in 'bearing the reproach of Christ.'" Sarney, too, would soon desert the cause, and become, in Charles Wesley's words, "entirely estranged by the offense of the cross." The piety of the Holy Club was not the piety of the diaspora mission. Böhler remained at Oxford, setting up societies among the awakened students, while Wesley returned to London.[38]

His trip to Germany was an introduction to the diaspora system that lasted more than three months. In June, he left England in a party of eight, five Englishmen and three Germans, led by Johann Töltschig, whom Wesley knew from his time in Savannah. In Holland, they visited the diaspora base at Ysselstein and spent time "in hearing the work which God is beginning to work over all the earth; and in making our requests known unto Him, and giving Him thanks for the mightiness of His kingdom." In Amsterdam, on a Monday, they visited one of the societies. Their host was the Mennonite minister, a Mr. Decknatel. The hymns that were sung had been taken from the Herrnhut hymnal and translated by Decknatel into Dutch. Sixty members attended the meeting. The next day, Wesley was taken to visit another society, "where were present about the same number." In the Wetterau he visited societies that had been formed in the neighborhood of Marienborn, where Zinzendorf maintained his residence-in-exile. Eighty-eight of the brethren, Wesley wrote, "praise God with one heart and one mouth at Marienborn; another little company at Runnerburg, an hour off; another at Büdingen, an hour from thence; and yet another at Frankfort [sic]."[39] At Herrnhut, Wesley attended meetings of the bands. Whether these bands belonged to the Herrnhut settlement or to the neighborhood is not clear. At Jena, he was introduced to members of the student society. "Those of them to whom we were recommended behaved as brethren indeed. Oh may brotherly kindness, and every good word and works, abound in them more and more!" On leaving Herrnhut, Wesley paid visits to the Lutheran ministers who presided over diaspora societies at Neukirch and Hauswalde. A second visit was made to the society at Frankfurt, "where one of the brethren from Marienborn offered free redemption, through the blood of Christ, to sixty or seventy persons."[40] What Wesley encountered on his trip to Germany, however, was not the Moravian church. In 1738, Lissa, Poland was the only place in Europe where one could attend a public service conducted by a Moravian clergyman in accordance with Moravian ritual. In the eyes of the Moravians Wesley met, the Moravian church was an institution that existed only for missionary purposes abroad, in places where no other church existed. What Wesley saw was the diaspora system. It is this, and the zeal it encouraged, that he eagerly responded to. "The spirit of the Brethren is beyond our highest expectations," he said. "Young and old they breath nothing but faith and love at all times and in all places. I do not concern myself with smaller points that touch not the essence of Christianity, but endeavor (God being my helper) to grow up in these after the glorious examples set before me." By the time Wesley left Herrnhut in August, he had resolved to take up diaspora work himself. "I would gladly have spent my life here; but my Master calling me to labor in another part of His vineyard . . . I was constrained to take my leave of this happy place. . . . Oh when shall THIS Christianity cover the earth, as the 'waters cover the sea'?"[41]

Wesley reached London on the 16th of September and began diaspora work the next day. "I began again to declare in my own country the glad tidings of salvation." On the 17th, he expounded "the Holy Scripture to a large company in the Minories." The next day, he "went to a society in Bear Yard," and on the 19th, he "spoke the truth in love at a society in Aldersgate Street." On the 21st, Wesley went to a society in Gutter Lane, on the 23rd to a society identified as Mr. Extell's. These societies were all located in London. On the 26th, he spoke to "a small company" at Windsor. On October 6, he returned to London and spoke to a society at Wapping. On the 9th, he set out for Oxford, where he spoke and expounded to three societies. On the 14th, he wrote to Herrnhut reporting his progress. "We are endeavoring here . . . to be followers of you, as you are of Christ. . . . we now have eight bands of men, consisting of fifty-six persons; all of whom seek for salvation in the blood of Christ." On the 18th, he returned to London and met a society at Westminster, whose membership consisted "chiefly" of soldiers. On 10 November, he was back again in Oxford, where he addressed "a little company"; and on December 10, he spoke to a society that met at the premises of a Mr. Fox.[42] No more society visits are mentioned until the new year. On 25 February, Wesley met four assemblies in London: "About three hundred were present at Mr. Sim's; then I went to Mr. Bell's, then to Fetter Lane, and at nine to Mr. Bray's where also we only wanted room." On the following day he had three more engagements, "in the Minories at four, at Mrs. West's at six, and to a large company of poor sinners in Gravel Lane (Bishopsgate) at eight. On March 2, he returned to Oxford. This was done on the advice of his brethren at Fetter Lane. There he met societies at Mr. Fox's and Mrs. Compton's. "The power of our Lord was present at both, and all our hearts were knit together in love." Efforts were made to set up a society in Reading, but this was thwarted by the intervention of the parson. "The enemy was too vigilant," Wesley wrote.[43]

In the spring, Wesley shifted his activities to Bristol. This was done at the initiative of George Whitefield, who had been working as an itinerant in the West Country. In March, Whitefield called on Wesley for help in setting up societies on the Moravian pattern. "Many are ripe for bands. I leave that entirely to you—I am but a novice; you are acquainted with the great things of God." The request had to be approved by Fetter Lane. "If the brethren after prayer for direction think proper, I wish you would be here the latter end of next week." That Whitefield also worked on behalf of Fetter Lane is clear from his correspondence with Wesley.[44] Whether Wesley would go was put to the lot. The use of the lot was a Moravian practice. "And by this," wrote Wesley, "it was determined I should go." Bristol is remembered as the beginning of Wesley's career as a field preacher. "At four in the afternoon, I submitted to be more vile, and proclaimed in the highways the glad tidings of salvation, speaking from a little eminence in a ground adjoining to the city." Field-preaching had nothing to do with Moravianism; but looking after societies did, and this Wesley continued to do. On 4 April, he visited the village of Baptist Mills. "In the evening three women agreed to meet together weekly." It was done with the same intention as those at London— viz. to confess their faults one to another, and pray one for another that they may be healed." Later that same evening, four young men agreed to meet, "in pursuance of the same design." Back in the city the next day, "I began at a society in Castle street expounding the

Epistle to the Romans; and the next evening, at a society in Glouces-
ter lane, the first Epistle of St. John." Two days later, "at Weavers' Hall
also I begun expounding the Epistle to the Romans; and declared that
gospel to all which is the 'power of God unto salvation to every one
that believeth.'"[45]

Wesley's mission followed the Moravian pattern. How far it was
carried out in collaboration with the Moravians, we cannot tell. Wesley started the mission immediately after returning from Germany,
where he may have been encouraged by the Moravians. Fetter Lane
was not the first diaspora society to embark on a mission in its own
neighborhood. The Lutheran pastor, Johann Steinmetz, ran a small
network of societies in Bayreuth. The first society set up in Regens-
berg was founded by the diaspora society in Augsburg. The Basel
society served as the center of a large network which, in time, included twenty-six villages and had a membership of nearly 500 brethren.[46] Some of the societies Wesley visited in London and Bristol
were perhaps Anglican foundations, the "religious societies" set up
in accordance with rules recommended by Anthony Horneck and
Josiah Woodward, which had flourished at the beginning of the
century. Parish institutions, their membership was restricted to
churchmen, and their proceedings were controlled by the parson.
Their piety was ascetic, not evangelical. Nothing linked them together into a working connection. In the 1730s, they may have experienced a renaissance. The supposition of this renaissance is
important to the argument that Methodism sprang from a background
in Anglican piety. The evidence of society activity in this period,
however, is largely associated with the Fetter Lane diaspora mission.
For all that is known, the societies Wesley visited in London and
Bristol may owe their existence to Moravian initiative. It is yet to be
shown that any of them were parish societies of the old pattern. That
some of them were is not impossible.[47]

In Germany, diaspora workers did not object to visiting societies
that others had founded.[48] It is unlikely that all of them were Anglican
religious societies. As members of a parish society, it is hard to
count the soldiers whom Wesley met in Westminster. The Moravian
diaspora mission in England goes back to 1728. That year, three
workers were sent: David Nitschmann, Johann Töltschig, and Wenzel
Neißer. In 1734–35, Spangenberg was living in London, making
preparations for the Moravian mission to Georgia. In 1737, Zinzendorf visited London and in 1738, Peter Böhler, Georg Schulius, Abra-

ham Richter, and Wenzel Neißer. All these visits were short; none had diaspora work as its primary purpose. This, however, was how the diaspora mission was often carried out. Like Böhler (and, later, Molther), the missionary did his work "on the fly," making contacts where he could, forming societies where they were to be formed, then moving on in the expectation that in time another worker would follow. Each did what he could in the time he had. In the Württemberg diaspora, Lange based his work on a set of contacts Zinzendorf had made during an earlier tour. We know that several societies were set up by Böhler and one each by Zinzendorf and Wenzel Neißer. It is a fair assumption that the other workers also made contacts and formed societies.[49]

A religious revival is like a political campaign: much depends on the advance work done. Before you start, you must know who your contacts are, where they can be found, and what they can do to put you in touch with others who want to hear what you have to say. A dozen people cannot be brought together in the same room to talk about salvation unless advance preparations have been made. Wesley himself made no preparations. He started his mission in London within twenty-four hours of getting back from Germany. Who gave him the names and addresses of the meetings he visited over the next three months? Who put him in touch with the soldiers' society in Westminster? Who told him about the society that met at Windsor? In 1738, the Moravians were the only people we know of who ran an itinerant mission. Therefore the possibility cannot be excluded that Wesley acted on information from the Moravians, or that the societies he visited formed part of an emerging diaspora network.

For the rise of Methodism, however, the derivation of the societies Wesley visited in 1738 is not the question. Even if by, some strange improbability, all were Anglican in origin, what is not Anglican and what cannot be accounted for in the contexts of Anglican religious societies, is Wesley's status. In no case was he the parish minister— not in Oxford, Reading, Windsor, Wapping, Westminster, Bishopsgate, Bristol, or anywhere else. With or without the permission of the parsons, Wesley persisted in the direction of societies that met in parishes that belonged to other men. In doing so, he acted as a Moravian diaspora worker. From the beginning, parsons objected. "You think," he wrote to one of them, "I ought to sit still; because otherwise I should invade another's office if I interfered with other people's business and intermeddled with souls that did not belong to me." The problem here was not field-preaching; that was yet to come. The problem was meeting irregular societies. "You accordingly ask," he said,

> how is it that I assemble Christians who are none of my charge to sing psalms and pray and hear the Scriptures expounded; and think it hard to justify doing this in other men's parishes, upon catholic principles.

Wesley goes on to make the statement that provides the text of his epitaph in Westminster Abbey: "I look upon all the world as my parish; thus far I mean, that in whatever part of it I am, I judge it meet, right, and my bounden duty to declare unto all that are willing to hear the glad tidings of salvation." This passage was taken directly from the Moravians. Zinzendorf also claimed the world as his parish, and did so in the very terms used by Wesley: "Ein Profet hat seine Pfarre in der ganzen Welt." What Zinzendorf says in German, Wesley says in English.[50]

Methodists are not wrong when they think of Wesley as their founder. Without his resolution and energy, Methodism could not have maintained itself as a movement separate from Moravianism, on the one side, and Evangelicalism, on the other. Innovativeness, however, should not be confused with originality. Wesley never hesitated to appropriate the ideas of other men and use them for his own purposes. In matters of literature and scholarship, he was an admitted plagiarist. The commentary he printed in a collection of hymns published in 1767 was taken from William Jones's *Catholic Doctrine of the Trinity* (1756). His attack in 1775 on the American revolution, *A Calm Address,* comes from Samuel Johnson's *Taxation no Tyranny* (1775).[51] In both cases, Wesley plagiarized without acknowledgment. Often no effort was made to hide the debt. The 1771 edition of his collected works reprints extensive extracts taken from William Law, Jonathan Edwards, John Norris, and John Goodwin.[52] The largest work Wesley published was *A Christian Library.* Published in 1750 and running to fifty volumes, it was an anthology that claimed in its subtitle to offer "extracts from, and abridgements of, the choicest pieces of practical divinity, which have been published in the English tongue." The selection of authors ranged from the apostolic fathers to such modern divines as Tillotson, Baxter, Pascal, Cudworth, and Fénelon.[53] Even writing on his own account, it was often difficult for Wesley to put aside his authorities and speak in his own voice. The *Survey of the Wisdom of God in the Creation* was published in 1763. This actually is a translation and reworking of a Latin treatise by the Pietist theologian, Johann Buddeus, which Wesley admits in his introduction. The commentary Wesley adds to the text is itself taken from other authors.[54] The same talent for imitation manifests itself in the *Explanatory Notes upon the New Testament* (1755). Here, Wesley largely draws on Johannes Bengel's *Gnomon Novi Testamenti* (1742). In the introduction, Wesley states that Bengel's text was incorporated into his own "without scruple."

A debt to other authors is acknowledged: John Guyse, John Heylyn, and Philip Doddridge. Wesley confessed that he had thought of identifying the precise passages he had borrowed:

> It was a doubt with me for some time, whether I should not subjoin to every note I received from them, the name of the author from whom it was taken; especially considering I had transcribed some, and abridged many more, almost in the words of the author.

The impulse was resisted. "Upon farther consideration, I resolved to name none, that nothing might divert the mind of the reader from keeping close to the point in view, and receiving what was spoke, only according to its own intrinsic value."[55]

Wesley was not the sort of person who piqued himself on his originality. When he wished, the work of other people was appropriated and used for his own purposes. This imitativeness is evident in his leadership of the Methodist revival. Modeling the Methodist connection on the Moravian diaspora was not out of character. Sometimes he acknowledged his plagiarisms, and sometimes he did not. In the case of the Moravians, the indebtedness was denied. *Plain Account* was written to mislead. The reader is encouraged to think that Methodism had emerged spontaneously and owed nothing to its Moravian background. Wesley lied when he wrote that, in founding Methodism he had no idea where he was going and followed no plan. He lied when he attributed the origin of the Methodist constitution to a succession of accidents and improvisations. Why he did so must remain a matter of conjecture. Perhaps the bitterness of the Fetter Lane schism made it hard to tell the truth. It is not easy to acknowledge a debt to people one has come to hate.

Wesley, however, did not lie for reasons of vanity. The Moravians were not dropped merely to magnify his own importance. What Wesley stresses in the *Plain Account* is not his importance but his unimportance in the emergence of the Methodist constitution. Nothing was premeditated. Everything happened by accident. Nothing occurred at his initiative. It was others who innovated, and he who followed. Wesley's motive in writing the *Plain Account* was to ward off censure and blame. He ends by professing his wish "to have a 'conscience void of offense toward God and toward man.'"[56]

As a clergyman in the Church of England, Wesley did not admit that he had deliberately set up an association that was schismatic in its tendencies. Nor did he admit that its constitution was derived from a foreign, possibly heretical model. Wesley wrote *Plain Account* as a piece of working propaganda. It is not the recollection of an old man eager to claim his rightful place in history: it was written in 1748 and published in 1749. Intended for an Anglican audience, it takes the form of a public letter addressed to Vincent Perronet, an Evangelical parson. Perronet's parish at Shoreham, in Kent, was one of the few places where Methodist preachers could count on a favorable welcome. In the pamphlet, Wesley is talking to friends and allies in the Church of England. He speaks not as the ex-Moravian itinerant who claims the world as his parish but as the ordinary churchman who responds to the duties of his calling and to the opportunities that providence offers. In this context, his Moravian past is something he would rather not talk about. Wesley's pretension to Anglicanism increases over time. In the *Plain Account,* Methodism is a spontaneous growth; in later statements, it is a development from his association in the Holy Club at Oxford.

The fact is, Methodism in its ecclesiology owes nothing to the Church of England. Like Moravianism, Methodism was intended to complement the work of other denominations. Wesley entertained no wish to challenge the Church of England or even to break with it. Zinzendorf, in Germany, pretends to be a good Lutheran, Wesley, in England, a good Anglican. Neither, however, cared to obey the church to which he professed fidelity. Each worked in the diaspora mission and was inspired by a conception of churchmanship that had little to do with Lutheran or Anglican orthodoxy.

4

Enlightenment

ZINZENDORF WAS BORN IN 1700, WESLEY IN 1703. BOTH BELONGED TO THE EIGH-teenth century and were contemporaries of Voltaire and David Hume. As citizens of this century, the claims of Voltaire and Hume are acknowledged and those of Zinzendorf and Wesley often denied. They preached faith in an age of skepticism. The revival they led takes place at the wrong time. "The terrified crowds" that listened to Wesley, says Peter Gay, "would have been at home in twelfth-century Chartres."[1] The philosophers "who commented so sardoni-cally on their terror would have been strangers there: the enchant-ment of the supernatural had gone from their lives."[2] Leslie Stephen denied all affinity between the revival and the enlightenment. "There could scarcely be said to exist even the relation of contradiction." Wesley "could as little appeal to the reason of Hume's scholars as Hume could touch the hearts of Wesley's disciples."[3] Gay and Ste-phen are intellectual historians and speak as representatives of the enlightened. As a church historian speaking for the faithful, Martin Schmidt does not essentially disagree. Schmidt's Wesley also op-poses the main tendencies of eighteenth-century thought. The "Leit-motiv" of Wesley's life was restoration of the primitive church. What attracted him to the Moravians was their ability to live like Christians in apostolic times. Herrnhut realized the life of the "Urgemeinde."[4] Here we see reflected a tendency to overstate the opposition between knowledge and faith. Today, we often suppose that those who know do not believe, and those who believe do not know. However, in practice, Jerusalem can have something to do with Athens.

In the eighteenth century, the Enlightenment and the Revival were events that coincided in time and, to some extent, overlapped in content. Zinzendorf's favorite author was the French skeptic, Pierre Bayle. In Bayle's quarrel with the Calvinist zealot, Pierre Jurieu, Zin-zendorf favored the skeptic and condemned the zealot. "It is better that the Jurieus of this world take me for a Bayle, than the Bayles for a Jurieu," Zinzendorf said. His fascination with the *Dictionnaire historique et critique* (1702) shocked the devout. The Pietist Conrad Dippel did not understand how anyone with a taste for godly things could waste time with such a "nasty work." It was "full of abominations." Bayle was a "swine," an "atheistical charlatan." The *Dictionnaire* was Zinzendorf's "vademecum"; Dippel thought he took it everywhere on his travels and relied on it for spiritual nourishment.[5]

Wesley was perhaps more widely read than Zinzendorf and certainly more circumspect in his choice of favorite authors. A list of what he read between 1725 and 1734 shows an interest in theology, philosophy, literature, and church history. It also shows an interest in natural science. He read Edmund Halley, Robert Boyle, Isaac Newton, and Francis Bacon along with several treatises on medicine. The interest in science sprang in part from an interest in natural theology. Wesley read the works that proved the existence of God from the constitution of nature: John Ray's *Wisdom of God Manifested in the Works of Creation* (1691) and William Derham's contribution to the Boyle lectures: *Physico-Theology, or a Demonstration of the Being and Attributes of God from his Works* (1713). He also followed experimental work in electricity and later bought himself an electrical "apparatus" which he used in his amateur medical practice. Wesley's faith in electricity as a cure-all was boundless. "We know it is a thousand medicines in one, in particular, that it is the most efficacious medicine in nervous disorders of every kind."[6] With enthusiasm, he read the results of Benjamin Franklin's experiments in America. "What an amazing scene is here opened for after-ages to improve upon." In 1760, Wesley published *The Desideratum; or Electricity made Plain and Useful.* This reported the latest research in electricity and recommended its application to medicine. Whatever else he believed in, Wesley believed in science, in its truth and in its beneficence. In the *Desideratum* he urged scientists to press on with their research:

> And if a few of these lovers of mankind . . . would only be diligent in making experiments, and setting down the more remarkable of them, . . . I doubt not but more nervous disorders would be cured in one year, by this single remedy, than the whole English *Materia Medica* will cure by the end of the century.[7]

In its rejection of metaphysical rationalism, the revival overlapped with the Enlightenment. Wesley and Zinzendorf agreed in their dislike of Leibniz, a view they presumably shared with Hume and certainly with Voltaire. Referring to Leibniz in his quarrel with the Newtonians, Wesley wrote:

> So poor a writer have I seldom read, either as to sentiment or temper. In sentiment he is a thorough fatalist. . . . And his temper is just suitable to his sentiments. He is haughty, self-conceited, sour, impatient of contradiction, and holds his opponent in utter contempt.

Zinzendorf said that he had read Leibniz's *Theodicy* (1710) with as much profit as a play by Racine or Corneille. Referring to Leibniz's principle of sufficient reason, Zinzendorf wrote: "Would to God, those who wearily blunder around in causation, should stumble into the sea of God's mercy. Then they would see the cause in the effect."[8] The revival presupposed an empiricist epistemology. Seeking the assurance of salvation, not in the conclusions of understanding but in the testimony of the heart, the believer had to rely on the veracity of his sensations.[9] Zinzendorf and Wesley both make explicit appeal to the authority of the senses. Before the Aldersgate experience, Wesley proved his lack of faith from evidence of what he felt: "By the most infallible of proofs, inward feeling, I am convinced . . . of unbelief." Supposing that belief manifests itself in love, he wrote: "I feel this moment I do not love God; which therefore I *know* because I *feel* it. There is no word more proper, more clear or more strong."[10] In the Aldersgate conversion, he again appealed to feeling. "I felt my heart strangely warmed. I felt I did trust in Christ, Christ alone for salvation." Wesley identified sensible inspiration as the "main doctrine of the Methodists." It was "the substance of what we all preach." It was a point he defended in controversy:

> I know the proposition I have to prove, and I will not move an hair's breadth from it. It is this: "No man can be a true christian without such an inspiration of the Holy Ghost as fills his heart with peace and joy and love, which he who perceives not has it not." This is the point for which alone I contend; and this I take to be the very foundation of Christianity.[11]

For Zinzendorf, feeling is the "concomitant" of evangelical truth; in it, we find the proof for our possession of faith. "As long as you do not feel, you have not tasted the word of God," he wrote, quoting Luther. For Zinzendorf, how one felt was the ultimate principle on which all arguments depended for their validity. *Es ist mir so,* or *that is how I feel* served as a sort of war cry. "Take away this, and we turn into complete skeptics and cannot know whether we really exist." This was what Scripture meant when it spoke of giving one's heart to God. "The effect of this is: that is how I feel, *ita sentio.*"[12]

In making the appeal to sensation, Zinzendorf and Wesley participated in the eighteenth-century reaction against Descartes. Descartes had subordinated feeling to reason. Information gained through the senses was fallacious and unreliable; real knowledge was to be obtained by the operation of reason working on the ideas that are innate in all. For Descartes, knowledge that is true approximates the knowledge we possess in mathematics, where what we know comes through reason alone and owes nothing to the senses. The attack on Descartes and the rehabilitation of the senses began with John Locke in England and was continued by George Berkeley and David Hume. In France, it was led by Voltaire and Condillac, in Germany by Christian Thomasius. In Germany, the reaction against Descartes was less complete than it was elsewhere. Leibniz and Christian Wolff defended an epistemology that is essentially rationalist. Zinzendorf, however, came under the influence of Thomasius, not Leibniz and Wolff. He and Thomasius knew each other and corresponded. In the introduction to *Der teutsche Sokrates,* Thomasius is referred to as the "world-famous jurisconsult and philosopher." It was Zinzendorf's differences with Thomasius over theology that prompted him to write *Der teutsche Sokrates.*[13] What they disagreed about, however, did not extend to matters of epistemology. Zinzendorf was not well read in philosophy, and it is hard to find him considering epistemological issues independently of their theological implications. In his theology, however, a strong empiricist bias manifests itself. In the 1720s, he had made inquiries about one of the feral children discovered in the forests of eighteenth-century Europe. It was literally a child of nature who was supposed to have grown up free of all human contact and instruction. Zinzendorf wanted to know whether the child showed any sign of innate ideas. The particular idea he was interested in was the idea of God which Descartes presumed all of us possess. Like a good empiricist, Zinzendorf wanted to establish a posteriori whether something might be known a priori. Alas, the examination proved nothing. "Every effort was made," Zinzendorf was told,

> to teach the boy to speak . . . so that something could be found out about his *Notionen.* But up to now, he has hardly learned enough to ask for

what he needs. His hearing is good; his articulation is more like barking than proper speech. He cannot answer any questions and his memory is not even as good as an animal's. In short, there is little about him that is human or rational. And there is no hope that he will ever learn anything.[14]

Wesley knew more philosophy than Zinzendorf, and it is possible to reconstruct his epistemology in detail. As an undergraduate, Wesley had read Locke's *Essay concerning Human Understanding,* and, as a fellow at Lincoln, he took up an abridgement of it with his students. He repeatedly recommended the *Essay* as suitable reading to devout Methodists and in the 1780s had lengthy extracts republished in the *Arminian Magazine.*[15] "From a careful consideration of this whole work," he said, "I conclude . . . it contains many excellent truths, proposed in a clear and strong manner, by a great master both of reason and language. It might be of admirable use to young students if read with a judicious Tutor." Like Locke, Wesley denied that things could be known in their nonperceptible characteristics. "For many ages," he said, "it has been allowed by sensible men, *Nihil est in intellectu quod non fuit prius in sensu.* . . . All the knowledge which we naturally have is originally derived from our senses." This was agreed to by "all impartial persons." Even the obvious truths that we know as soon as we begin to reason originate in experience. "The knowledge even of those is not innate, but derived from some of our senses."[16] A distrust of reason is a persistent characteristic in Wesley's thought. Knowledge consisted not in what the mind understood but in what it experienced. "What pretence have I," Wesley asked, "to deny well-attested facts, because I cannot comprehend them." He distinguished between the intelligibility of an idea and its truth. "Those who will not believe anything but what they can comprehend, must not believe that there is a sun in the firmament. . . . They must not believe that they have a soul; no, nor that they have a body." Empiricism colored the way Wesley looked at everything. In his manual on medicine, *Primitive Physic* (1747), Wesley stands as the champion of experience and the opponent of speculation. Good medicine proceeded by trial and error, bad medicine by rational theorizing.[17] It was the sufficiency of sensible evidence that justified his belief in ghosts. In the case of ghosts, as in the case of murder, the testimony of competent witness proved the reality of what he believed: "The testimony of unexceptionable witnesses fully convinces me both of the one and the other." Accepting ghosts on empirical grounds, however, he refused to accept any account of their nature on grounds that were not empirical. This was his complaint against Joseph Glanvill's *Sadducismus Triumphatus*, published in 1681:

All his talk of "aerial and astral spirits" I take to be stark nonsense. Indeed, supposing the facts to be true, I wonder a man of sense should attempt to account for them at all. For who can explain the things of the invisible world but the inhabitants of it?

In the end, the real nature of visible things was no more accessible to human reason than the true nature of Glanvill's spirits. When Wesley published his *Survey of the Wisdom of God* (1763), he disclaimed all knowledge of things in their nonempirical characteristics.

I endeavor throughout not to account for things, but only to describe them. I undertake barely to set down what appears in nature; not the cause of those appearances. The facts lie within the reach of our senses and understanding; the causes are more remote. That things are so, we know with certainty; but why they are so, we know not. In many cases we cannot know; and the more we inquire, the more we are perplexed and entangled.

In natural philosophy, Wesley thought, the best we can do is to describe and classify what we learn through the senses. Things in their metaphysical nature lie beyond the reach of our understanding.[18]

Wesley liked Locke and was unstinting in his recognition of Locke's originality, particularly in his theory of knowledge. "I think that point, 'that we have no innate principles,' is abundantly proved, and cleared from all objections that have any shadow of strength. And it was highly needful to prove the point at large . . . as it was at the time an utter paradox both in philosophical and religious world." He defended Locke against such critics as John Norris and Thomas Reid, who objected to the supposition that what the mind perceived was perceived through the medium of ideas. "Why," Wesley asked, "should any one be angry at his using the word 'idea' for whatever is the object of the mind in thinking?" The idea was an indispensable postulate for the explanation of thought. "To talk of 'thinking without ideas' is stark nonsense. Whatever is presented to your mind is an idea; so that to be without ideas is not to think at all. Seeing, feeling, joy, grief, pleasure, pain are ideas. Therefore to be without ideas is to be without either sense or reason."[19]

In his empiricism, Wesley ultimately derives from Locke. But it was not Locke so much as Peter Browne who worked the direct and immediate influence on Wesley's thought. In Wesley's day, Browne's *Procedure, Extent, and Limits of Human Understanding* figured in the deist controversy as one of the main defenses of revelation. What distinguishes Browne's argument is the extreme empiricism of its premises. Browne went beyond Locke and denied that the mind could perceive any sensible evidence of its own existence. Here, perhaps, Browne resembles David Hume. For Browne, all the ideas the mind could possess were those of external sensation. The fact and manner of the mind's existence could be known only through the perception of things external to itself.[20] It was a case not of "to be is to be perceived" but of "to perceive is to be." Browne may have anticipated Hume in denying that the mind could possess any a priori knowledge of causation.[21] Browne published *Limits of Human Understanding* in 1728, shortly before Wesley took up residence at Lincoln, and it made an immediate and lasting impression on him. At Lincoln, Wesley wrote a lengthy abstract of the work and showed it around to his friends. This was later published as an appendix to the *Survey of the Wisdom of God* (1777). Wesley used *Limits of Human Understanding* in the education of his preachers and recommended it to Methodists for private reading.[22] Browne's *Limits of Human Understanding* had been written explicitly for the refutation of deism; Locke's *Essay* had not. For this reason, Wesley thought more highly of Browne than of Locke. Browne's book was "in most points far clearer and more judicious than Mr. Locke's as well as designed to advance a better cause."[23]

Zinzendorf and Wesley were influenced by empiricism in how they thought about religion. Both condemned speculative theology and denied that God could be known a priori. Nothing, they believed, could bridge the chasm separating the finite creature and the infinite creator. "A being exists," said Zinzendorf,

> that needs nothing else. It is so boundless in its immensity that, whether we call it God or nothingness, it is something we cannot understand. It cannot be done, even if we commanded the cleverness of all the philosophers who ever lived. It is not wisdom but madness to venture into the infinite convolutions of God's mind.

Zinzendorf's God is utterly incomprehensible. He may legislate laws, but Himself is bound by none. He may break every rule He institutes.

All the preestablished harmonies, Zinzendorf said in allusion to Leibniz's metaphysics, exist merely at the pleasure of God. "He can crumple up what we call heaven and earth . . . and throw it away, if he wishes, like a scrap of paper." Moreover, what might be learned through the exercise of reason was irrelevant to what the Christian needed to know.[24] "Religion must be the sort of thing, that can be mastered not through abstractions but through sensation." Were this not so, children and the feeble-minded, who lack the capacity to grasp abstractions, might never be saved.[25]

In admitting the argument from design as proof for the existence of God and the beneficence of His nature, Wesley went beyond Zinzendorf, but he agreed with him in rejecting a priori theology. Where Zinzendorf dismissed Leibniz, Wesley dismissed rationalist theologians such as Samuel Clarke and Andrew Ramsay. Referring to Ramsay's *Philosophical Principles* (1749), Wesley wrote: "The treatise . . . gave me a stronger conviction than ever I had before of the fallaciousness and unsatisfactoriness of the mathematical method of reasoning on religious subjects." In Wesley's view, Clarke and Ramsay studied divinity upside down. "All this is beginning at the wrong end; . . . we can have no idea of God, nor any sufficient proof of His very being, but from the creatures . . . the meanest plant is a far stronger proof hereof" than all of the arguments of Clarke and Ramsay. Wesley discouraged "curious metaphysical disquisition" about matters where revelation was obscure. Reason was not to be consulted in vain efforts to make the Trinity intelligible:

> What have you or I to do with that difficulty I dare not, will not, *reason* about it for a moment. I believe just what is revealed, and no more. But I do not pretend to *account* for it, or to solve the difficulties that may attend it. Let angels do this, if they can. But I think they cannot.[26]

Here, Wesley follows the lead of Peter Browne in the latter's *Limits of Human Understanding*. Browne argued that the facts of revelation prescribe the limits of Christian belief and understanding. Revealed facts bear an analogical relationship to the realities of God, but what these realities truly were, apart from man's comprehension of the analogy, formed no part of the faith the Christian had to believe or understand. Here, Browne taught Wesley to make a distinction between believing something and understanding what it meant. Wesley acknowledged the debt in a sermon on the Trinity: "That great and good man, Dr. Peter Browne . . . has proved at large that the Bible does not require you to believe any mystery at all. The Bible barely requires you to believe such facts; not the manner of them. Now the mystery does not lie in the *fact,* but altogether in the *manner.*" Wesley asserted his belief in the Trinity but disclaimed all understanding of its real constitution. "I have no concern with it: it is no object of my faith: I believe just so much as God has revealed and no more."[27] Wesley's reliance on the revealed word of Scripture owes as much to philosophical skepticism as it does to credulity.

Zinzendorf shared Wesley's dislike of speculative theology. What we find in Zinzendorf, however, and do not find in Wesley, is a radical emphasis on the atonement as a perceptible event in history. It is this that led Zinzendorf to adopt the *Versöhnungslehre,* and it is what distinguishes Moravianism from Methodism in their respective theologies. Zinzendorf was a Christocentrist. In his conception of the Trinity, he magnified the importance of the Son in relation to the Father and the Holy Ghost. The godhead itself was an unknowable abstraction and not the proper object of Christian worship. From the Bible, it is known that godhead, in its essence, is the Father, the Son, and the Holy Ghost. "Beyond this we know nothing," said Zinzendorf. It is folly to sort out the constituents and try to understand how they relate to each other. A Moravian prayer somewhat irreverently dismisses the deity of speculative abstraction: "We honor your divine majesty, your inaccessibility, your primal, uncreated, endlessness. But we heed you not. Whatever you are, it is nothing that we can apprehend with our minds and senses or know how to deal with."[28] The believer's connection with the Trinity runs through Christ, and Christ alone. Christ is often seen as the mediator who restores us to a proper relationship with God, the Father.

For Zinzendorf, the only relationship that counts is that with Jesus. As Beyreuther puts it, in Zinzendorf, "our communion with Christ is not the means to communion with God, it is communion with God." *Christusgemeinschaft* and *Gottesgemeinschaft* are the same thing. The Trinity exists, to be sure, but Christ acts as *Amtsgott,* the official deity. He is virtually God, and it is with him that our business is done. He represents the godhead to mankind. On Zinzendorf's supposition, it is Christ as God who acts as creator and manifests himself to the Jews as Jehovah in the Old Testament. In the incarnation, He acts as our savior and redeemer. What we know of God, the Father, and the Holy Ghost is known only through him. Zinzendorf called him a compendium or guidebook that teaches us about the Trinity.

Our relationship to the Father and the Holy Ghost is subordinated to our relationship to the Son. It is through Him that our obligations to the Father and to the Holy Spirit are satisfied. "They deal *menschlich* with us, because we belong to the Son. To get to the Father and the Holy spirit, we need go no further than Jesus." Whoever knows Jesus as his creator and savior can number himself among the saints in heaven and yet know nothing about God, the Father, and God, the Holy Ghost.[29]

What distinguishes the Son from the Father and the Holy Ghost in the end, is his perceptibility. In him, the word became flesh. "The Saviour has taken on something, that the Father and the Holy Ghost did not take on." Emphasis on the real humanity of Jesus was the *Hauptmaterie* of Moravian christology. Jesus appeared on earth, "not mystically, not spiritually, not sacramentally, but *corporaliter,* with flesh and blood like any other child."[30] In suffering on the cross, what He did is to be understood as the action of a real person. "He did not triumph as God but did it as a man, and with the same powers that we possess. God sustained Him; Christ sustains us. He had no strength, other than the strength we receive from him." Belief in Christ starts with belief in the facts of His temporal life. This must be apprehended like the truth of any other historical fact. "For salvation . . . what is needed is an historical belief and nothing else." It is all "a matter of history, and I can think of no easier way to salvation than an historical belief" in Jesus. It is this that effects our rebirth. Once the reality of this truth is perceived, its force is irresistible. "That is the nature of history: it grasps the heart."[31]

What worked here was the reality of a fact that could be perceived and understood empirically. It was knowable in a way that the conclusions of speculative theology were not. In their worship, Moravians sought to re-imagine the life of Christ in all its historical detail. This did not mean that they perceived truths not revealed in Scripture. Zinzendorf thought of the atonement as something that had to be visualized before it could be understood. In Wilhelm Betterman's words, it was "ein Bild, nicht ein Begriff." Like Doubting Thomas, Zinzendorf insisted on knowing the truth in its palpable reality. "Like that dull-witted disciple, I thrust my finger into the side-wound of the Saviour. It is there that my soul came to believe."[32] In Methodism, on the other hand, it was not the Savior's side-wound the believer was asked to examine, but the believer's own state of mind. Wesley's preoccupation was not historical but psychological; this is the point at issue in the debate between Wesley and Zinzendorf over the *Versöhnungslehre*. On both sides, speculative theology is rejected. On both sides an appeal is made to the authority of sensible evidence, but it was to sensible evidence of different things. For Zinzendorf, the appeal was to what happened in the past, whereas, for Wesley, it was to what happened in the present in the heart of the believer.

The Methodist experience consisted in part in the perception of the emotional reactions or effects that manifest the possession of faith. Using biblical terms, Wesley called these manifestations the fruits of faith, the fruits of the spirit, or the testimony of the believer's spirit.[33] These included peace, joy, and love; sometimes, meekness, gentleness, and righteousness were added to the list.[34] "These . . . inward fruits of the Spirit . . . must be *felt* wheresoever they are; and without these, I cannot learn from Holy Writ that any man is 'born of the Spirit.'" This experience constituted evidence of faith. In defense of Methodist conversions, Wesley challenged an opponent: "What excuse have you for not being convinced that *they* have *faith*, who have the fruits which nothing but faith can produce?"[35]

These manifestations were necessarily perceptible. "It cannot be in the nature of things, that a man should be filled with this peace and joy and love . . . without perceiving it as clearly as he does the light of the sun." Love and joy and peace "are inwardly felt or they have no being." The insistence on their perceptibility predates Wesley's own conversion. In 1725, he wrote, "Surely these graces are not of so little force, as that we can't perceive whether we have them or no: and if we dwell in Christ . . . certainly we must be sensible of it."[36] The fruits were received as the supernatural gifts of the Holy Ghost. Yet the perception of these gifts did not presuppose the believer's possession of supernatural faculties. In this respect, the believer experienced only the effects of inspiration, not their cause. He felt peace, love, and joy but not the influence of the Holy Ghost itself. That such effects were divinely inspired, the believer could learn only from Scripture. "Whoever has these inwardly feels them," Wesley said; "if he understands his Bible, he discerns from whence they come. Observe, what he inwardly feels is these fruits themselves; whence they come he learns from the Bible." To account for their perception, Wesley presupposed nothing more than believers' ordinary faculties of reflection and self-consciousness. The Christian knew that he loved God in the same way he knew he loved any mortal. Indeed, the Christian knew of his love of God in the same way he knew whether he was hot or cold—that is, by sensation or by feeling. "How does it appear to you," Wesley asked, "that you are alive, and that you are now in ease and not in pain?" "Are you not immediately conscious of it?" On the same evidence, we must know of our feelings toward God. "By the same means you cannot but perceive if you love, rejoice, and delight in God. By the same you must be directly assured if you love your neighbor as yourself."[37]

What the fruits of faith provided was indirect proof of the believer's salvation. Scripture told the believer that whoever possessed the fruits was a child of God; inward consciousness assured him that he possessed them; thereupon, he might logically conclude that he was a child of God. To this was added a direct proof that the believer was told to expect. Independently of the logical proof, the direct evidence told him of God's forgiveness.[38] The direct evidence cannot simply be understood as an expression of the believer's confidence in the favor of God. By the very nature of the thing, the assurance of pardon had to precede the believer's knowledge and confidence: "A man cannot have a child-like confidence in God till he knows that he is a child of God." Wesley supposed, further, that the direct witness was, for the believer, a perceptible experience. Scripture told him that direct testimony occurred; logic told him it must occur in a perceptible form. "Am I not to perceive what is testified? . . . Then it is not testified at all. This is saying and unsaying in the same breath. Or am I not to perceive that it is testified to my spirit? Yea, but I must perceive what passes in my own soul!"[39]

In perceiving the fruits of faith, Wesley assumed nothing more than the believer's natural powers of self-consciousness, but in the perception of the direct witness, he had to suppose the operation of a special faculty, a spiritual sense only the believer could possess. Wesley first referred to the spiritual sense in the *Earnest Appeal to Men of Reason and Religion* (1743). He denied that the mind possesses innate ideas; what it knows comes from the senses. In the case of spiritual truths, however, the physical senses are inadequate. For the perception of spiritual truths, spiritual senses are needed. Without these, the believer can no more perceive the direct testimony of the Spirit than a blind man could perceive color.[40] Through the act of the Holy Ghost, the believer acquired the spiritual sense in his regeneration. Indeed, for Wesley, regeneration is to be understood largely as the reception of the spiritual sense. He compared the unawakened Christian to the child in the womb. Both lack the sensitive faculties needed to perceive the reality that surrounds them. For both, it is the awakening of the senses that distinguishes the birth.[41]

Christians who lack spiritual senses cannot themselves be expected to know what it is the believer experiences. In Wesley's view, to explain the direct witness to the unregenerate was like explaining sight to the blind or sound to the deaf:

> He who hath that witness in himself, cannot explain it to one who hath it not: Nor indeed is it to be expected that he should. Were there any natural medium to prove, or natural method to explain, the things of God to unexperienced men, then natural man might discern and know the things of the Spirit of God.

In the end, the spiritual sense of the believer constitutes the essence of his faith. The spiritual sense "is with regard to the spiritual world, what sense is with regard to the natural. It is the spiritual sensation of every soul that is born of God." For Wesley, this was no mere figure of speech, but a fundamental definition of what he thought faith was. "Faith implies both the perceptive faculty itself and the act of perceiving God and the things of God." Wesley resisted all attempts to identify faith with truth independently of its perception. Faith is not just what believers believe. "No it is no; no more than the light which a man sees is his sight."[42] Faith is a function of the human psychology.

When Wesley undertook to account for faith as a sensible experience, he claimed no credit for originality; indeed, he asserted the contrary. Understandably, his strategy was to insist that it was he who was traditional and orthodox, and his opponents who were not. On different occasions, he appealed to different authorities in defense of his orthodoxy: Puritan divines like Richard Sibbes, William Perkins, and John Preston; and reformers on the Continent such as Martin Luther and Philipp Melanchthon. In controversy with William Warburton, he appealed to the Homilies of the Church of England.[43] However, one ally Wesley never cited—or, at least, never cited with approval—was David Hume. When Wesley thought of Hume at all, it was of Hume the infidel and skeptic—"the most insolent despiser of truth and virtue that ever appeared in the world" and "an avowed enemy to God and man, and to all that is sacred and valuable upon earth."[44]

Nevertheless, there is a correspondence between Wesley and

Hume to be seen in their theories of belief. Neither thought of belief as the assent of the understanding; for both, it was a matter of feeling. "Belief," wrote Hume "is more properly an act of the sensitive than of the cogitative part of our natures."[45] In neither case is belief something the human mind could create at will. For Wesley, the mind can believe only in collaboration with the Holy Ghost. "Is it in your power," he asked, "to burst the veil that is on your heart and to let in the light of eternity? You know it is not. You not only do not but cannot (by your own strength) thus believe. The more you labour so to do, the more you will be convinced, 'it is the gift of God.'"[46]

For Hume as well, the origins of belief were external to the will. "Belief consists . . . in something, that depends not on the will, but must arise from certain determinate causes and principles, of which we are not the masters."[47] In Wesley's case, the external force was God, in Hume's it was nature. Hume's empiricism prohibited the exclusion of any conceivable source for the sensations the mind felt. Even without the guidance of scripture, Hume had to admit the sensations of belief could be effected by a supernatural agency.[48] Both Hume and Wesley faced the same difficulty when they tried to identify what it was that manifested belief to the mind of the believer. In the end, neither could specify the characteristics of the sensation whose existence they posited. Wesley shunned any philosophical discussion of the point. "He who hath that witness in himself, cannot explain it to one who hath it not: nor is it expected that he should."[49] To know what the direct witness was required the proper spiritual senses. Hume was no more successful: "I confess that 'tis impossible to explain perfectly this feeling or manner of conception." Belief defied definition:

> Were we to attempt a *definition* of this sentiment, we should perhaps find it a very difficult, if not an impossible task; in the same manner as if we should endeavour to define the feeling of cold or passion of anger, to a creature who never had any experience of these sentiments.[50]

For both Hume and Wesley, then, only a believer could tell what another believer felt. The two theories of belief are not identical, of course. First, Hume's argument is that mind feels *that* it believes; Wesley's is that it feels *what* it believes. Of the two, Wesley's is the less tidy and elegant. It forces him to postulate a sensation to correspond with everything that is believed in the mind; whereas Hume's theory does not. In other words, Hume can account for the belief of a man who believes a lie; Wesley cannot. Second, Wesley's argument accounts only for the saving faith of a Christian. He said nothing about belief in general.

The likelihood that Hume influenced Wesley in his epistemology is remote. The similarity of their theories owes more to their common intellectual inheritance than to the chance of any direct connection. Both are indebted to the philosophical empiricism that dominated eighteenth-century thought. In his conception of faith as a sensitive power of the mind, Wesley, however, is closer to Hume than he is to any of the Christian empiricists of the eighteenth century. John Locke and Peter Browne viewed faith as an assent to a probable truth; neither thought of it as a faculty or power.[51] Here, Wesley was on his own. To be sure, he drew on a long tradition of Christian thought that distinguished between faith and assent. He was not the first to think of faith either as a supernatural event or as a sensible experience.

The *Bußkampf* piety he learned from the Moravians taught Wesley a psychological conception of conversion. In the entire process, the convert's attention is directed to nothing but his own state of mind. The spiritual sense that Wesley supposed, however, represents a peculiarly eighteenth-century solution to an epistemological problem. What Wesley did in divinity is similar to what Francis Hutcheson did in ethics. Both postulated a sense to account for the knowledge they supposed the mind to possess. Wesley's spiritual sense is the theological counterpart to Hutcheson's moral sense. Perhaps the similarity did not escape Wesley's notice. He disliked Hutcheson and thought that the point of the latter's moral philosophy was to exclude God from the explanation of right and wrong. "God has nothing to do with his scheme of virtue from beginning to end." In Wesley's eyes, Hutcheson's moral theory was "Atheism all over." Yet, in its more formal and, philosophically, more important elements, Wesley agreed with Hutcheson that morality is the domain of human feeling, not of human understanding. In the very passage where Hutcheson was condemned for atheism, Wesley accepts the existence of Hutcheson's moral sense. In his *Thoughts on Taste* (1780) Wesley asks: "Is there not a kind of internal sense, whereby we relish the happiness of our fellow-creatures, even without any reflection on our own interest, without any reference to ourselves?"[52]

In a sermon, Wesley alludes to Hutcheson in describing the faculty that perceived the fruits of the Spirit. "Some late writers indeed have given a name to this, and have chose to style it a *moral sense.*" Wesley preferred the term *conscience*, but the difference was nominal. It remained "a faculty or power implanted by God in every soul ... of perceiving what is right or wrong in his own heart or life."[53] In supposing the existence of a spiritual sense to account for what is learned through the witness of the Spirit, Wesley did nothing in divinity that he did not countenance in moral philosophy.

Natural jurisprudence formed the second point of contact between Enlightenment and Revival. Wesley and Zinzendorf both supposed that associations derived their authority from consent. In their ecclesiology, both were contractualists. Zinzendorf had studied law at Wittenberg and knew about natural law as a technical system of jurisprudence. He had read Hugo Grotius and it is a fair presumption that he also had read Christian Thomasius. He believed people possessed rights. Serfdom existed in Saxony but not at Herrnhut. The Moravian refugees who took up residence there settled as free tenants. Serfdom was an institution Zinzendorf disapproved of.[54] It was on the ground of natural right that he justified the formation of private religious societies. Here, he differs from Spener, who had invoked the priesthood of all believers, thus implying a supernatural justification. This, Zinzendorf rejected. Assemblies for religious purposes were to be defended on the same grounds as assemblies for nonreligious purposes. Also, if an assembly convened for a religious purpose proved disorderly or seditious, it might be prohibited like any other assembly.

The right of association had nothing to do with orthodoxy. Those who were mistaken in their beliefs possessed the same right to meet as those who were not mistaken. "Even if it is wrong, the honest man must never sacrifice his conscience to the power and pleasure of another." Moravians supposed that their societies existed through the favor of providence and that, to this extent, they possessed a supernatural status. In this world, however, their supernatural status was not the basis on which they claimed the right to exist. "The rights that any worshipful company or society enjoys everywhere under the protection of the magistrate are also due to the small congregation that belongs to Jesus," wrote Spangenberg.[55] In 1727, the residents of Herrnhut constituted themselves as a proper *Gemeine,* or congregation. This was effected through a contract, the *Brüderlicher Verein und Willkür,* which every member signed. Founded on the mercy of God, "in christo," this society had the purpose of promoting brotherhood among its members. Offices were instituted on the model of the primitive church: elders, exhorters, overseers, and visitors for the sick. Of course, there is a radical difference between the primitive church of the first century and the Herrnhut society of the eighteenth. The latter derives from a social contract, whereas the former does not. The hand is the hand of Paul; the voice is the voice of Rousseau.[56]

Although the terms of association vary over time and place, contract as a basis of membership persisted in Moravianism. In England, members pledged themselves to a later version of the "Brotherly Agreement." Swearing fidelity to the Augsburg Confession, they promised to educate their children in Moravian schools and not to set up in business or marry without the society's permission. Contract was extended even to mission stations in the New World. At Gnadenhütten, Pennsylvania, for instance, Indian converts were admitted to membership under the terms of a promise.[57]

The *Brüderlicher Verein und Willkür* was the instrument that constituted the Moravian society; it did not constitute the Moravian church. In its form, this was a supernatural foundation that owed its existence to the consecration of Zinzendorf and David Nitschmann as bishops in the old Moravian succession. With its own episcopacy, the new church could pretend to a clerical legitimacy that stretched back to the first apostles. And, with its own orders, the church could carry on missionary work abroad. The restored hierarchy, of course, owed nothing to contract. In theory, at least, the Moravian church claimed a supernatural authority that passed from bishop to bishop by consecration and from the bishops to the subordinate clergy by ordination. This succession was something the Moravians advertised, particularly in their relationship with the Church of England. Addressing the Archbishop of Canterbury, Zinzendorf asserted his full apostolical status, referring to himself as "We Lewis by Divine Providence, Bishop, Liturgus, and Ordinary of the churches known by the name of the Brethren; and, under the auspices of the same, Advocate during life, with full power over the Slavonic Unity; Custos Rotulorum . . . and Prolocutor both of the general synod and of the Tropus of instruction." In Georgia, Wesley attended the ceremony in which Anton Seifart was ordained by David Nitschmann.

> The great simplicity as well as solemnity of the whole, almost made me forget the seventeen hundred years between, and imagine myself in one

of those assemblies where form and state were not, but Paul the tent-maker or Peter the fisherman presided, yet with demonstration of the Spirit and of power.[58]

Moravian bishops exercised their apostolic functions with less so-lemnity than Wesley imagined. In Georgia, Nitschmann ordained Friedrich Martin in the Virgin Islands. Unable to get there, Nitsch-mann laid hands on Martin through the mail. "Let the spirit of witness descend upon you, Friedrich Martin," Nitschmann wrote in his letter. "Thou shalt baptize, celebrate holy communion, bless marriages, confirm, and do everything else, named and unnamed that belongs to a servant of the Church." In 1742, George Schmidt, working in South Africa, received his ordination in a letter sent to him by Zin-zendorf.[59] The Brethren, in fact, did not attach importance to apos-tolic succession, nor did they suppose a real distinction in status between the laity and the clergy. In their view, church ceremonies and institutions were matters that might vary according to time and place.

The new Moravians took from the old Moravians "whatever suited us best in our present circumstances," Spangenberg wrote. Apostolic succession was not insisted on as a test of church legitimacy. Mora-vian missionaries were ordained to avoid giving offense, not to vali-date their sacraments. In principle, a congregation might entrust the administration of its sacraments to whomever it chose.[60] In conversa-tion with Wesley in Georgia, Spangenberg actually denied the reality of apostolic succession. The lack of apostolic legitimacy was one of the complaints Wesley made against the Moravians in the schism. "Your Church discipline is novel and unprimitive throughout," he said.

> Your Bishops, as such are mere shadows, and are only so termed to please those who lay stress upon the Threefold Order. . . . The ordination (or whatever it is termed) of your Eldest plainly shows you look upon Episcopal ordination as nothing. . . . The constitution of your Church is indeed congregational, only herein differing from others . . . that you hold neither this nor any other form of Church government to be of divine right.[61]

Like the Moravian society, the Moravian church, as an institution, derived its authority from its members.

Wesley's attack on Moravian ecclesiology formed part of a long letter of complaint that he sent to Herrnhut in August 1740, two weeks after he left Fetter Lane. In 1744, the letter was published in the journal that covered the period of the schism. Intended to give Wesley's side of the story in the schism, the journal opens with a preface specifically addressed to the Moravians. The letter of August 1740 was printed as a summary statement of what Wesley thought the issues really were. At the end he wrote,

> Thus I have declared, and in the plainest manner I can, the real contro-versy between us and the Moravian Brethren: an unpleasing task, which I have delayed as long as I could with a clear conscience. But I am constrained at length nakedly to speak the thing as it is, that I may not hinder the work of God.

Again, Wesley's recollection cannot be completely trusted. In its pub-lished version, the letter makes no reference to Moravian ecclesiol-ogy. The passage was suppressed in which he disputed the validity of Moravian ordination and accuses the Moravians of denying divine right. The revision is referred to in an introduction where he tells the reader that two or three "less material paragraphs" had been omitted.[62] What mattered in 1740, when Wesley broke with the Mora-vians, mattered less when he defended himself in 1744. In the inter-val, he changed his mind on the question of church legitimacy. In 1740, it is important, in 1744 it is not. In 1740, the Moravians lack apostolic succession and do not think their church exists by divine right. In 1744, the defect in their legitimacy is overlooked. The prin-ciples of divine right and apostolic succession no longer have to be asserted. The fact is, these were principles Wesley could not assert in 1744, at least not in public. In forming the Methodist Connexion, he acted outside the Church of England and, in a sense, acted in defiance of its bishops. In 1744, it would have been absurd to object to Moravian orders, when he did not obey the presumably legitimate authorities within his own church.

Whether Wesley cared much about apostolic legitimacy even in 1740 is a matter of doubt. From his days in Georgia, he knew that the Moravians did not insist on it, yet he continued to work with them. Apostolic legitimacy was certainly something he discounted in 1744. It was not until the next decade, however, that this was made known to the world. In 1753, Wesley issued the next installment of his journal. In the entry for January 1746, he reports reading Peter King's *Inquiry into the Constitution of the Primitive Church* (1691). Presbyterian in its implications the work argues that early Christianity recognized no difference in authority between priests and bishops.

"In spite of the vehement prejudice of my education," Wesley wrote, "I was ready to believe that this was a fair and impartial draught; but, if so, it would follow that bishops and presbyters are (essentially) of one order, and that originally every Christian congregation was a church independent on all others!" In 1756, he invoked the authority of Edward Stillingfleet, who argued against episcopal government as a necessary institution existing by divine right. "This opinion (which I once heartily espoused)," Wesley wrote, "I have been heartily ashamed of ever since I read Dr. Stillingfleet's *Irenicon.* I think he has unanswerably proved that neither Christ or His Apostles pre-scribed any particular form of Church government, and that the plea for the divine right of Episcopacy was never heard of in the primitive Church."[63] Wesley agreed with King and Stillingfleet, but it was after, not before, his conversion from high episcopacy that he read them and invoked their authority.

Wesley's conception of church government reflects the individual-ism of eighteenth-century thought. In their authority, he believed, churches owe nothing to the truth of their doctrine. Wesley did on occasion cite article nineteen of the Thirty-nine Articles. This he did in *Earnest Appeal.* This article stipulates orthodoxy as the mark of a valid church: "The visible Church of Christ is a congregation . . . in which the pure Word of God is preached." It is sometimes sup-posed that article nineteen reflects Wesley's own convictions on the matter, but it does not. *Earnest Appeal* was a controversial work addressed to Anglicans; in it, Wesley argued ad hominem, "I was there arguing with every man on his own allowed principles, not contesting the principles of any man."[64] With reference to article nineteen, he wrote, "The definition which I occasionally cite shows nothing of my sentiments on that. . . . They may be strict or loose, right or wrong." In his sermon "Of the Church," article nineteen was abandoned. "I will not undertake to defend the accuracy of this definition."[65] The fact is, Wesley no more regarded orthodoxy as a mark of the church than as a test of membership in the Methodist Connexion. Not only was orthodoxy unimportant for Methodism, it was unimportant for Christianity. "Orthodoxy, or right opinions, is at best but a very slender part of religion," he said, "if it can be allowed to be any part of it all." Someone might sincerely be orthodox and still lack the faith that saves: "He may not only espouse right opin-ions, but zealously defend them . . . he may think justly concerning the incarnation of our Lord . . . and every other doctrine contained in the oracles of God . . . and yet it is possible he may have no religion at all, no more than a Jew, Turk or Pagan." Someone might, in principle, be quite unorthodox, yet still possess saving faith. "Persons may be truly religious, who hold many wrong opinions. Can any one possibly doubt of this, while there are Romanists in the world?" If orthodoxy was not essential to salvation, it was, a fortiori, not essential to the constitution of a valid church. Catholics subscribed to false doctrine, but this did not excommunicate them. "Neither would I have any objection to receive them, if they desired it, as members of the Church of England." Justification by faith was a doctrine whose supposition was crucial to the Methodist revival. It was a doctrine Wesley constantly taught. Justification, however, required no one's assent to the doctrine's validity. Someone might be justified and yet deny the very doctrine that explained his salvation. "But, if so," Wesley asked, "what becomes of *articulus stantis vel cadentis ecclesiae.*"[66]

As a society, Methodism claimed for itself no authority in the sanctity of its membership. Members were not a gathered body that excluded all but experienced believers. In Congregationalism, the member was admitted as a visible saint; in Methodism, he came as an acknowledged sinner. The point in joining Methodism was to gain the faith that saved, which does not mean, however, that every Methodist was presumed to possess it. Wesley never thought of the Society as a congregation of believers. He did not accept election, irresistible grace, or final perseverance. The Methodist saint could always lapse, in which case the grace he enjoyed would be lost. Even if Methodism had begun as a society of believers, Wesley could claim no assurance in doctrine that it could persist as such. From its foundation, we know, Wesley looked on Methodism as a mixed association whose ranks included members in all states of spiritual development: believers and nonbelievers, justified and unjustified. Under the rules of the Society, someone might be justified and still forfeit membership. Believers who belonged to the bands also were required to attend their classes together with nonbelievers. "If you constantly meet your band," he warned the believers, "I make no doubt that you will constantly meet your class; indeed, otherwise you are not of our Society. Whoever misses his class thrice together thereby excludes himself, and the preacher that comes next ought to put out his name." Getting into heaven and remaining in good standing as a Methodist were not the same thing.[67]

Wesley assumed a distinction between particular congregations and the universal church. Membership in the latter was determined by the possession of faith and extended "to all nations and all ages." It included "the holy angels" and "all who were departed in . . . faith and fear." The universal church existed "as to the very essence of it" as a body of believers. "No man that is not a Christian believer can be a member of it." It was necessarily an invisible institution.[68] A body that included the living, the dead, and the holy angels was not the Methodist society, nor did Wesley ever claim that it was. "I do not think . . . the People called Methodists . . . to be *the True Church of Christ*. For that church is but one, and contains all the true believers on earth." Wesley never supposed that membership in temporal churches should be limited to real believers. Temporal churches and the universal church of Christ were different things. He supposed that nonbelievers might receive the sacraments. The Lord's Supper was a "converting ordinance" from which nonbelievers might benefit.

> No fitness is required at the time of communicating, but a sense of our state, of our utter sinfulness and helplessness; every one who knows he is fit for hell being just fit to come to Christ in this as well as all other ways of His appointment.

A church existed for the sake of sinners, and sinners were entitled to share in its membership. Sinners, moreover, might direct its proceedings. Communion, for instance, could be administered by nonbelievers: "The reason is plain, because the efficacy is derived, not from him that administers but from Him that ordains it. He will not suffer his grace to be intercepted though the messenger will not receive it himself."[69]

The right to teach did not derive from possession of faith. Wesley repeatedly attacked the claim that only those who were saved could profitably preach. The case for Methodists remaining in the Church of England rested on the supposition that the infidel parson might benefit his congregation. Wesley put the argument on the strongest possible hypothesis: "What if I were to see a Papist, an Arian, a Socinian, casting out devils? If I did, I could not forbid even him without convicting myself of bigotry. Yea, if it could be supposed that I should see a Jew, a Deist, or a Turk, doing the same, were I to forbid him . . . I should be no better than a bigot still." His own authority as a teacher owed nothing to his status as a believer. Wesley denied that he taught anything as a result of inspiration. "I am ready

to give up every opinion which I cannot by calm, clear reason defend," he said. Nor did the possession of faith exempt the believer
from the need for human instruction. "As 'all men have not faith,' so
all believers have not wisdom."[70] Exemption could not be claimed
even by those of the faithful who had pressed on to sanctification.
"There is no saint upon earth whom God does not teach by man."
On this point he reprimanded Thomas Maxwell, one of Wesley's first
preachers and the leader of a holiness rebellion in the Methodist
Society: "I dislike your saying that one saved from sin needs nothing
more than looking to Jesus; needs not hear or think of anything else;
believe, believe is enough . . . and that he cannot be taught by any
person who is not in the same state." With reference to the Ranters
of the seventeenth century, the same point was made in his *Plain
Account of Christian Perfection* (1777): "To imagine none can teach
you, but those who are themselves saved from sin, is a very great
and dangerous mistake. . . . No; dominion is not founded in grace,
as the mad men of the last age talked."[71]

Methodism claimed no ecclesiastical status or supernatural identity in its association. Nothing exists corresponding to the Congrega-
tionalist covenant whereby members collectively incorporate
themselves into a spiritual body asserting the powers of a church.
Wesley had devised a covenant service, but this did not pretend to
incorporate anything. It was a devotional ceremony in which the
worshipers covenanted not with each other but with God. Methodists
get themselves saved, one at a time, and in this reflect the individual-
ism of the eighteenth century. The rules and procedures that were
adopted were not justified as obligatory institutions. They were not
represented as things prescribed by Scripture or that possessed any
merit apart from their utility. Wesley described them as "little pruden-
tial helps." They could be abandoned or altered as circumstances
required; they were not "essential" or of "divine institution." When
Wesley formed Methodists into classes and bands, he did not claim
an authority in Scripture. "These are man's works, man's building,
man's invention." What recommended them was their utility in reason and experience. They were introduced "in order to apply
the general rules given in Scripture according to particular
circumstances."[72]

Like any private association, Methodism found its authority in the
consent of its members. Wesley was a clergyman in the Church of
England, yet he denied that his ordination gave him any right to

direct the Methodist movement. Referring to his authority as leader
of the Connexion, he wrote: "I did not exert it as a priest, but as one
whom that Society had voluntarily chosen to be at the head of them."
When members were expelled for a fault, Wesley acted not as a
priest but as a layman. "I took upon me no other authority . . . than
any steward of a Society exerts by the consent of the other members.
I did neither more nor less than declare that they who had broken
our rules were no longer of our Society."[73] It was the terms of consent
that governed his relationship with the members and with the itinerant preachers. It was the terms of consent he appealed to in denying
the right of preachers to administer the sacraments. He always distinguished between what a layman might do and what one of his
preachers might do as a Methodist. In the latter case, it was the terms
of membership that were decisive. "You . . . aver that you have a
right to administer the Lord's Supper," he wrote to a preacher, "and
that you ought to administer it among the Methodists. If the assertion
was proved, I should deny the consequence." Whether his preachers
acted as priests or as laymen depended ultimately on what Wesley
wanted them to do. In Scotland, he allowed them to act as priests,
wear bands and gowns, and administer the sacraments. When the
same men returned to England to work in English circuits, however,
they returned as laymen. North of the Tweed, Wesley addressed them
as *Reverend,* south of it as plain *Mister.* "We are to be just what we
were before we came to Scotland," one of the returning preachers
complained, "no sacraments, no gowns, no, nothing at all of any
kind whatsoever." The preacher continued: "Even the pope himself
never acted such a part as this. What an astonishing degree of power
does our aged father and friend exercise!" The difference was, the
papacy believed in the reality of priesthood, and Wesley did not. As
officers of the Society, Wesley's priests acted under its rules. Priests
and preachers served on the same understanding. They had agreed
to work under his direction, and this determined what their powers
were. "For, supposing (what I utterly deny)," Wesley told them, "that
the receiving you as a Preacher, at the same time gave an authority
to administer the sacraments; yet it gave you no other authority than
to do it, or anything else, *where I appoint.* But where did I appoint
you to do this? Nowhere at all. Therefore, by this very rule you are
excluded from doing it."[74]

Wesley's objection to lay administration did not spring from in-
tense concern with the validity of the sacraments. If anything, his

attitude toward the sacraments was a sensible, unsuperstitious one. True religion resided in the heart of the believer, "not in any *outward thing;* such as *forms,* or *ceremonies,* even of the most excellent kind." Forms and ceremonies could reflect inward piety; they could encourage devotion. They could even be of divine institution, yet they did not represent the essence of faith. "True religion does not principally consist therein; nay, strictly speaking, not at all. . . . The religion of Christ rises infinitely higher, and lies immensely deeper, than all these." Ceremonies, "subservient to true religion," were "good in their place." Regarded as aids to human frailty, any objection to them was unjustified. "But let no man carry them farther. Let no man dream that they have any intrinsic worth; or that religion cannot subsist without them. This were to make them an abomination to the Lord." Christians were commanded to receive the sacraments, and obedience was, in a sense, beneficial. Yet the benefit was not effected through the agency of the rite. "The virtue in the sacraments doth not proceed from the mere elements and words, but from the blessing of God in consequence of his promise to such only as rightly partake of them, and are qualified for it." In the case of baptism, Wesley thought the form of the sacrament unimportant. It was a sacrament that could even be neglected. "You think the mode of baptism is 'necessary to salvation'," he wrote. "I deny that even baptism itself is so; if it were every Quaker must be damned, which I can in no wise believe."[75] Baptism was neither spiritual regeneration nor the cause of spiritual regeneration; it was a sign of regeneration and, as such, something distinct from what it signified. "What can be more plain, than that the one is an external, the other an internal, work; that the one is a visible, the other an invisible thing, and therefore wholly different from each other?—the one being an act of man . . . the other a change wrought by God in the soul." One could occur without the other: "They do not constantly go together. A man may be 'born of water' and yet not be 'born of the Spirit.' There may sometimes be the outward sign, where there is not the inward grace."[76]

In strict logic, Wesley had little cause to worry about the validity of the sacraments or whether they were administered by qualified priests. Because they were external ceremonies, the legality of their administration made little difference to their spiritual effect. It is possible that, in the early days, Wesley believed valid orders essential to the life of the church. In 1739, it was his ordination that he invoked when he was challenged by Beau Nash for preaching in the fields at Bath. Asked by what authority he preached, Wesley replied: "By the authority of Jesus Christ, conveyed to me by the . . . Archbishop of Canterbury, when he laid hands upon me." Eleven years later at Shaftesbury, when confronted with the same challenge, it was not his apostolic commission that Wesley invoked but his civil right: "While King George gives me leave to preach, I shall not ask leave of the mayor of Shaftesbury." In the interval between the two events, Wesley had set up a system of lay preaching. He could not assert his priesthood without disavowing the very preachers whom he had appointed. Priesthood ceased to be an essential qualification for the preacher. "I allow that it is *highly expedient,* whoever preaches . . . should have an outward as well as an inward call; but that it is *absolutely necessary,* I deny." In England, he persisted in refusing to allow his preachers to administer the sacraments. This reflects his wish not to break with the Church of England and turn Methodism into a dissenting sect; it does not reflect a sacerdotal conception of religion. For Wesley, what saved the sinner was not the sacrament, but the word. Priesthood played a subordinate—and possibly not indispensable—part in conversion. He permitted lay preaching be- cause, without it, "thousands of souls would perish everlastingly." He prohibited lay administration "because I do not conceive there is any such necessity for it; seeing it does not appear that, if this is not at all, one soul will perish for the want of it."[77]

In his conception of what constitutes a church, Wesley's thought ultimately is Latitudinarian. Wesley believed that God had willed men to be members of churches and that, to this extent, membership was not a matter of choice. "This is not the appointment of men, but of God. He saw it was not good for men to be alone, even in this sense." Yet, Wesley denied the existence of any visible church that could claim this membership as a right. His denial of authority extended even to the undivided church of antiquity. Wesley often professed admiration for primitive Christianity and sometimes cited its usages for controversial purposes. He spoke of Methodism as if it were a restoration of the primitive church. "I have not found any community who . . . come so near the Scripture plan, or so nearly answer the original design of a church, as the people called Methodists."[78] To him, Methodism was "the religion of the primitive Church, of the whole Church in the purest ages." Strictly read, Wesley supposed that the primitive church was little more than a lay association that conducted its business without the help of an ordained priesthood. In their determinations, the great church councils were "generally trifling, sometimes false, and frequently unintelligible or self-contradictory!" Not even the primitive fathers could be entirely relied upon. In controversy with Conyers Middleton, Wesley admitted that "some of these had not strong natural sense, that few of them had much learning." Whoever read them would "find many mistakes, many weak suppositions, and many ill-drawn conclusions."[79] Respect was due the fathers as witnesses to the authentic faith, not as authoritative teachers. Such men had been near contemporaries of Jesus and pupils of the Apostles. They "must have had a most comprehensive and perfect knowledge of the faith as it is in Jesus." In the end, Wesley recognized no church, whether ancient or modern, that could claim obedience in its jurisdiction. If submission to authority were required, then, Wesley declared, "I could be a member of no church under heaven. . . . I dare call no man Rabbi. I cannot yield either implicit faith or obedience to any man or number of men."[80]

Against the claim of church authority, Wesley asserted a right of private judgment that was absolute and uncompromising:

> Every man living, as a man, has a right to this, as he is a rational creature. The Creator gave him this right when he endowed him with understanding. And every man must judge for himself, because every man must give an account of himself to God. Consequently this is an indefeasible right; it is inseparable from humanity. And God did never give authority to any man, or number of men, to deprive any child of man thereof, under any colour or pretense whatever.

Here, Wesley is speaking the language of the eighteenth century; he is assuming the same jurisprudence that is assumed by Thomas Paine in the latter's *Rights of Man*. The churches that men belong to derive their authority from consent. They stand on the same right as any other association people chose to make for their common purposes. Essentially, the relationship that exists between pastor and Christians was a contractual one. "I cannot guide any soul unless he consent to be guided by me. Neither can any soul force me to guide him, if I consent not."[81] Once this consent is withdrawn, the church connection is dissolved.

Methodists and Moravians both appeal to the authority of contract in justifying their collective existence. In each case, they want to do their own thing in their own way. Theirs is a right every citizen can claim for private purposes. Moreover, it is a right that can be claimed without menace to public liberty. The Christian who demands religious freedom on the grounds of orthodoxy or sanctity disputes the freedom of everyone who does not share the same conception of orthodoxy and sanctity. This claim is necessarily theocratic, and its logic forces us to form churches that are Quaker-like or Catholic-like in their pretensions. No doubt, Methodists and Moravians thought they were orthodox and saintly, but their right to worship as they see fit is not based on this; it is based on a claim that concedes the same right to those who are unsaintly and unorthodox.

5

The Meaning of Methodism

METHODISM IS A DOCTRINE JOHN WESLEY PRESCRIBED. HOW THE DOCTRINE IS TO be read is a question that has divided historians. This division, however, does not extend to what it is they are referring to. In talking about Methodism, we are talking about Wesley. His importance lies in his leadership of a mass movement; it may, therefore, seem capricious to analyze his thought without reference to the beliefs of his followers. Indeed, sorting out what Wesley thought is crucial to understanding what was believed. Methodism never pretended to be a democracy in which everyone could have a say in deciding what was taught. In this respect, Wesley is the only one who matters; he is the only one who can speak for the movement in its entirety. As a system of belief, Methodism cannot be divorced from what he thought. Methodists joined the Connexion on his terms, and on his terms they might also be expelled. In their membership they received the right to have his counsel, directly or indirectly.

Wesley was the beneficial owner of every chapel in the Connexion; without his permission Methodists, as Methodists, could not be preached to. In this sense, he is the only spokesman eighteenth-century Methodism possesses. Moreover, it is his thought that we find difficult to understand. He wrote a great deal in defense of Methodism, yet, like all men of action, what he says is often unclear and incomplete. He wrote to persuade, not to explain. In discerning his basic premises, we may find that he is a hard author to read. Read him we must, however, if we are to decide what Methodism is and where it comes from. What the Methodist believes in practice is an important matter. It may or may not approximate the Methodism Wesley taught. But that is another question, one that cannot be addressed until we first decide what it is that is being taught.

The first thing that identifies Methodism is its insistence on evangelical conversion. Christians must be born again. Through the testimony of experience, they have to know they are born again; if they do not know this, they are not saved. This experience is effected through faith, not earned by the merit of our works or by the efficacy of the sacraments. It is Wesley's commitment to sensible conversion that distinguishes him from the nonevangelical clergy in the Church of England. It distinguishes Methodism from the piety of his years at Oxford, as well as the piety he learned from his parents. Other Anglicans before him perhaps recognized the necessity of evangelical conversion, but their influence is not evident in *Wesley's* background in the Church of England. In any reading of Methodism that stresses the importance of Wesley's Anglican antecedents, the importance of evangelical conversion in Methodism must be downplayed. In reality, it is asserted by him consistently from his own conversion in 1738 until his death. It is the first fact of Methodism, and something from which he never deviates. He insists on it in a sermon as late as 1788:

> "He that believeth," as a son (as St. John observes) "hath the witness in himself." "The Spirit itself witnesses with his spirit, that he is a child of God." "The love of God is shed abroad in his heart by the Holy Ghost which is given unto him."[1]

The point of the revival was to encourage Methodists to convert. The doctrine derives from German pietism, which Wesley learned about from his contact with the Brethren in Georgia. On this point, the evidence is abundant and conclusive. His quarrel with the Brethren in the 1740s did not arise because Wesley changed his mind. He did not revert to the High Anglican piety of his youth. Pietism was not cast aside in favor of Anglican sacramentalism or Anglican asceticism. The quarrel arose out of a difference over technique and method. In the 1730s, the Brethren had encouraged converts to proceed to faith through conviction of sin. In order to know that you were forgiven, you first have to know that you deserve damnation. This is what Wesley had been taught in Georgia. On the return voyage from Georgia, he experienced the anguish associated with the Pietist *Bußkampf;* at the Aldersgate assembly, he attains the *Durchbruch* whereby he knows of his salvation. In the Revival, Wesley urged others to seek salvation by using the same method. Wesley and the Methodists stick to this, whereas the Brethren do not.

In Moravianism, *Bußkampf* piety is superseded by the *Versöhnungslehre.* Evangelical conversion is still insisted on, but the way to get there is to stress the facts of our salvation, not the reality of our sinfulness. Perhaps the quarrel between the Methodists and the Brethren was inevitable; Zinzendorf and Wesley were good leaders but poor followers; nevertheless, the terms of their quarrel are important for the definition of Methodism. It is important to recognize that it was the Brethren who were innovating, not the Methodists. What was at issue was the need to inculcate in the convert a conviction of sin. This is what the Brethren had taught Wesley in the first place. In insisting on it, Wesley does not revert to the piety of his Oxford days. Oxford is a late invention which Wesley introduced into the history of Methodism. At the time of his quarrel in the summer of 1740, the appeal he made was to what he supposed was the authentic doctrine of the Brethren as it had been taught to him:

> I further assert, 'This I learned (not only from the English, but also) from the Moravian Church,' And I hereby openly and earnestly call upon that Church (and upon Count Zinzendorf in particular, who, I trust is not ashamed or afraid to avow any part of the gospel of Christ) to correct me, and explain themselves, if I have misunderstood them or misrepresented them.[2]

Wesley's insistence on evangelical conversion has often led people to think of Methodism as an eighteenth-century version of seventeenth-century Puritanism. Whether the Puritans taught evangelical conversion is not something that has to be decided here. It is clear that this is not the source Wesley got it from. His mother knew nothing of it. She denied that it was taught by Wesley's grandfather, Samuel Annesley, one of the Puritan martyrs who was ejected in 1662. Wesley's connection with the Puritans does not lie through his family. Nor does it lie through Oxford. An interest in Puritan divinity does not manifest itself until *after* he discovered evangelical conversion through the Moravians. His affiliation with German Pietism, we can prove; his affiliation with Puritanism, we cannot. That such an affiliation exists is improbable. Methodism and Puritanism are profoundly different. Puritans tended to be Calvinist in their theology and taught predestination. Wesley was anti-Calvinist and taught free will. The Puritans cared about doctrinal orthodoxy and define themselves in relation to formal creeds. Wesley dismissed creeds. Doctrinal orthodoxy, he said, is unimportant in the salvation of believers and the formation of churches. Furthermore, Methodism will not publish a confession of the Westminster kind or of any other kind. The failure to formulate a creed has led historians to think that

Methodism was confused and incoherent in its theology, but this misses the point. Creeds did not matter; what mattered was that the Methodists perceive the reality of their status. There are only two facts they had to know: first, that they are damned, and second, that they are saved. The first got them into Methodism, the second into heaven. In comparison to this, the rights and wrongs of theology were unimportant.

It is in its ecclesiology that the identity of Methodism stands out most clearly. Puritans and High Anglicans alike assumed the existence of legitimate churches but disagreed in how these churches were constituted. In the High Anglican tradition, it is through apostolic succession; in the Puritan, it is through the covenant of the believers. In both cases, the church is viewed as an institution claiming supernatural jurisdiction. The Methodist church is a club. It is a club, whether we think of it as a local society that meets weekdays and on Sunday sends its members to worship with non-Methodists in the parish church, or whether we think of it as an independent congregation that administers the sacraments and conducts its own Sunday service. In Methodism, we are saved one by one. To assist each other in the pursuit of salvation, we enter into associations. "A company of men joining together," wrote Wesley "we are accustomed to call a church." But this church itself was not of divine institution. It did not claim an authority that could prove itself either by Scripture or by tradition. People were allowed to form their own associations as they saw fit. In this, Wesley opposed both the High Anglicans and the Puritans in their conception of what a church ought to be. "Let me entreat you to speak plainly either one way or other," a Baptist critic wrote to Wesley.

> Prove to me, sir, by the Scriptures, that the Church of England, or the Methodists if you like it better, are rightly gathered and brought into a church state, and rightly governed; or else tell me the Scripture does not prove it. For either it does or it does not; if it does, then you can do it too; if it does not, then you can frankly own it, and acknowledge that you have been mistaken.[3]

This was a challenge that Wesley could not meet; Methodism derived its existence from the consent of its members, not from the authority of Scripture.

As a system of belief, Methodism is Latitudinarian in its theology and ecclesiology, and evangelical in its theory of salvation. Where it comes from, is the next question. If we look for models in England, it is hard to find anything that matches completely. In Puritanism, we may find evangelicals, but no evangelicals who are Latitudinarians; in Anglicanism, Latitudinarians, but no Latitudinarians who are also evangelicals. In Moravianism, we find both. Like the Methodists, the Moravians encouraged people to seek evangelical conversion; also like the Methodists, they attached little importance to the validity of doctrine or the legitimacy of church institutions.

Finding a counterpart to Methodism in England is even harder, especially if we insist on some evidence that Wesley came into contact with it and was actually influenced by it. His association with the Moravian diaspora, however, is abundantly documented in journals and letters. Subsequently, he denied its importance, but the denials are demonstrably false. Methodism as a finished and developed system owes little to its background in England. Deriving from German Pietism, it originated in Saxony and came to England by way of Georgia.

If Methodism is seen as something that originated in Wesley's conversion in 1738, the importance of the Moravians is hard to deny. Before the *Versöhnungslehre* was adopted, the Moravians encouraged their friends to work toward the very pattern of conversion that Wesley experienced. On shipboard during his return from Georgia, Wesley experienced the *Bußkampf* preliminary to conversion. This is the phase when the convert struggles against the force of his own sinfulness, and in struggling, repeatedly fails and recognizes that by himself he merits damnation. At this stage he perceives that nothing can save him but faith in Christ. It is this faith that he lacks. At Aldersgate in May, it is achieved. This is the Pietist *Durchbruch*, or breakthrough. Through experience, Wesley knows that he believes and that he is a child of God. To explain this crisis, we need not imagine that Wesley suffered a nervous breakdown that can be accounted for only through the insights of psychoanalysis. The truth is much simpler. The crisis of 1738 was, in a sense, self-induced. For two years Wesley had been living intimately with the Moravians. From the beginning, he regarded them as his spiritual directors. They instructed him in *Bußkampf* exercises, and in the end he gained the experience they had encouraged him to expect. Why one person responds to this kind of instruction, and another does not, may well defy historical explanation. But the content of the instruction owes nothing to the verities of psychoanalysis. Wesley did what he was told to do. He had a conversion experience on the pattern he was told to expect, and in leading the Methodist revival he goes on to instruct others in the *Bußkampf* exercises he himself had been instructed in.

Fashions in piety change, and in Georgia, Wesley had been introduced to something new which he responded to. To account for the Aldersgate experience, we do not have to suppose that he suffered a nervous breakdown. If he did, the evidence for the breakdown is largely limited to the conversion it is intended to explain. Apart from the conversion crisis, what strikes the reader of his journals and letters is Wesley's flatness and the stability of his emotional life. Here is no David Brainerd, alternating between periods of despair and periods of exultation. As in everything, Wesley is sober and business-like. He goes to Georgia and learns about a new method of conversion. He tries it out on himself. It works, and he decides to teach it to others. This is how Methodism got started.

The Methodist revival coincided with the Industrial Revolution in England. We are often tempted to think of it as something that emerges as a response to the realities of industrial life. E. P. Thompson sees it performing a "double service" and gaining adherents on both sides of the class struggle. For the factory owners and "their satellites," it provided "ideological self-justification." To Thompson, Methodism was the "pitiless ideology of work." Under its influence, business virtues and discipline were fostered. "Methodism was the desolate inner landscape of Utilitarianism in an era of transition to the work-discipline of industrial capitalism." At the same time it gave the working man an assurance of status and community. Methodism, "with its open chapel doors did offer to the uprooted and abandoned people of the Industrial revolution some kind of community to replace the older community-patterns which were being displaced." Here the disinherited of the industrial revolution "felt themselves to have some *place* in an otherwise hostile world."[4] What Thompson writes about the sociological function of Methodism may or may not be true, but it does not illuminate the origins of Methodism. Here, Methodism had nothing to do with the Industrial Revolution. It is part of a widespread Protestant religious revival, starting in the backwoods of Saxony and spreading to Georgia, where Wesley first makes contact with it. Its identity is decided before it reaches England. It is something that emerges at the periphery, not the center of eighteenth-century English society. There is nothing in it as a doctrine that can be understood as a response to the problems of industrialization.

Whether industrialization accounts for the success of Methodism is another question. To answer it, we shall have to count real Methodists in real places. Once this is done, we may well find that Methodism fared better in Birmingham than in, say, Rutland. This is what historians have supposed, and they are probably right. Methodism is one of the new things that happened in eighteenth-century England, and new things catch on better in towns than in the country. Methodism as a doctrine does not owe its identity to the realities of eighteenth-century English sociology; it is something people think. Whether it is coherent or incoherent, rational or irrational, progressive or reactionary, it is intelligible as a body of thought that exists in the minds of people. How they understand what they claim to think is the reality historians must deal with first. Methodism must be examined in its intellectual identity. As a system of thought, what does it look like in relation to other systems of thought? What is it that Methodists in eighteenth-century England supposed they believed? Until these questions are answered with some conclusiveness, our time is misspent in speculating on Methodism in its sociological or psychoanalytic origins.

The Methodism whose origins E. P. Thompson explains figures as a hybrid of Anglican and Puritan orthodoxies. It lacks logical coherence and cannot be accounted for in the context of intellectual history. Essentially, it is a social contrivance intended to work as a stratagem in the class struggle. Under its influence factory workers are sedated and factory owners animated and emboldened. The trouble with this theory is that the Methodism Thompson is talking about is not what Wesley taught—or, for all we know, what *any* Methodist believed. Real Methodism is intellectually coherent. In it, we see being worked out the implications of the Protestant Reformation. Once people decide that they are saved by faith, it is perhaps natural that they should ask how the possession of faith is testified to their minds. Once the authority of the priesthood is challenged, it is also natural that laymen acting as laymen should take charge of their own spiritual lives. To explain Wesley in relation to the class struggle is to talk about imaginary Methodism in an imaginary England. Real Methodism is ecclesiastical in its antecedents; and if social factors play a part in the formulation of its doctrine, these are more likely to be found in rural Saxony than industrial England.

Whatever difference Methodism makes to the course of English history is not a question that can be answered by analyzing Wesley's thought. Whether Methodism is liberal or conservative in its influence requires us to look at real Methodists in real places. How many were there? Where did they live? How many had the vote, and how did they use it? Looking at how Methodism got started, however, there is no need to think of it as necessarily counterrevolutionary in its implications. In its epistemology and ecclesiology, Methodism reflects the individualism characteristic of eighteenth-century thought. To see it as a reaction against the challenge of the Enlightenment is to misunderstand how it works in its essentials. Without eighteenth-century contractualism and eighteenth-century empiricism, the Methodist revival would been profoundly different in its identity. Too much attention is paid to the fact that Wesley opposed the American Revolution, too little to the fact that he himself conducted a revolution against the ancien régime in its ecclesiastical pretensions. The importance of Methodism as an innovation in eighteenth-century England is often denied.

J. C. D. Clark sees in Methodism evidence of the durability of the old order. It reflects the "intellectual vitality and strength of Orthodox churchmanship." It illustrates the ability of the established church "to put forth new branches." It draws on "the parent stem" for aspects of its "devotional practice and theology." It distinguishes itself from the parent "by different emphases on, or selections from, elements in the common tradition." It inherits "almost intact the political theology of mainstream Anglicanism."[5] Methodism, in fact, challenges the very tradition whose vigor it is supposed to testify to. In its pedigree, it owes nothing to High Anglican tradition; its ecclesiastical antecedents lie in Lutheran Pietism. The rapidity with which it spread may reflect the very reality Clark has striven to deny. This is the responsiveness of the times to change.

Eighteenth-century England was a dynamic world. Discipline and tradition were set at defiance. It was a time when people experimented, tried new things. They did it in how they managed their farms and conducted their business. They did it in the way they think about science, philosophy and government. They also do it in religion. Methodism is a novelty. It is an exotic importation, like tea, coffee, or cotton. It comes from abroad and catches on at home. Bernard Semmel has written of a Methodist *revolution* that transformed traditional English society. In this revolution, he says, lie the origins of nineteenth-century liberalism.[6] Whether Methodism causes liberalism is a question that requires us to look at Methodists in detail. But, in thinking of Methodism as a doctrine that is enlightened and individualistic in its implications, Semmel is closer to the truth than Clark. The rise of Methodism reflects the openness and liberality of eighteenth-century England, not the persistence a traditional, patriarchal system.

The genesis of Methodism is a much studied subject with an immense literature that grows year by year. A new edition of Wesley's collected works has been started under the general editorship of Frank Baker. In 1989, Henry Rack brought out *Reasonable Enthusiast: John Wesley and the Rise of Methodism,* probably the best book to date on the subject. And in 1995, Richard Heitzenrater published his *Wesley and the People called Methodists.* Rack and Heitzenrater both understate the importance of Moravianism in shaping Methodist thought and practice. This reflects a tendency in Methodist scholarship that can be traced back through Frank Baker, Albert Outler, Maximin Piette, Eli Halévy, and ultimately to John Wesley himself— at least to Wesley in his role as Methodism's first historian. Right or wrong, the general effect of this tendency is to give us a Wesley who looks somewhat un-Protestant: ascetic in his sanctity, sacramentalist in his worship, authoritarian in his ecclesiology. It is a Wesley who is fundamentally unlike the revival movement that springs from his leadership. Whatever Methodism may become, it is not a denomination that looks Catholic in any important sense. Moreover, imagining a Wesley who owes nothing to the Moravians makes it difficult to explain him as a man of even modest coherence in his thought. He must be—if we follow Outler, an eclectic, or Baker—a bundle of contradictions, or Thompson, a promiscuous opportunist. The Moravian Wesley makes better sense. He also is a man who is easy to account for in his eighteenth-century background. A Wesley who sometimes sounds like Cardinal Newman is not.

Not reading German, Methodist historians in the main know little about Moravianism. Here, the best example is Clifford W. Towlson in *Moravian and Methodist: Relationships and Influences in the Eighteenth Century* (1957). Towlson ignored the German literature and took the Moravian side of the story from Wesley. He relies on Wesley's testimony on the point where he is least to be trusted. Towlson is not alone here. Letting Wesley do our historical thinking for us has been a persistent fault in Methodist scholarship. The number of

historians who write on Methodism, and who read the German literature on Moravianism, is small. A recent exception is W. R. Ward, in
his *Protestant Evangelical Awakening,* published in 1992. Ward
places the origins of Methodism in the context of a general evangelical revival starting in Germany in the eighteenth century and spreading to England and North America. Like much of Ward's work, it is
immensely erudite, but, in its analysis, somewhat unclear. On the
relationship between Wesley and the Moravians, we are left where
we were: Wesley and the Moravians meet, they collaborate, they
quarrel, they part. How they stand in relation to each other in their
intellectual identity is not a question Ward addresses. His work sup-
poses some indefinite, unstated kind of origin for Methodism in Germany, but does not prove it or show what it was. Recently, J. C.
Podmore published two articles on the Fetter Lane society, that draw
heavily on Moravian archival evidence: "The Fetter Lane Society,
1738" (1988) and "The Fetter Lane Society, 1739–1740" (1990), in the
Proceedings of the Wesley Historical Society. He shows persuasively
that, in its origins, the society was Moravian, not Anglican. Whether
Moravianism influenced Methodism is not a question he answers—
or, indeed, needs to.

To find someone who knows German scholarship and is interested
in Methodism in its intellectual identity, we must turn to older authorities such as Martin Schmidt, in his *John Wesley: Leben und Werk*
(1953), and F. Ernest Stoeffler, in his 1976 essay, "Pietism, the Wesleys
and Methodist Beginnings in America." Primarily students of German
Pietism, Schmidt and Stoeffler are both interested in Methodism as
a manifestation of Pietism in England. Both argue for the importance
of Moravianism in Wesley's background. In neither case, however, is
the Moravian influence they argue for integrated into their analysis
of Wesley's thought as a whole. Guided perhaps by the main tendency of Methodist scholarship, each takes for granted a Wesley who
basically is incoherent in his thought: sometimes Catholic, sometimes Protestant, sometimes a dissenter, sometimes a churchman.
Moravianism is another ingredient added to the mix. Schmidt and
Stoeffler fail to see that Moravian influence in defining Methodism is
central and decisive. Two things are critical in the Methodist-
Moravian relationship, and these were missed: first, the diaspora
mission; second, the *Bußkampf.*

The Methodist Connexion represents a continuation of the Moravian diaspora mission, and Wesley merely carries on doing as a

Methodist what he had been doing as a Moravian diaspora worker. It is the diaspora mission that allowed him to evangelize England, free from denominational ties, and more important perhaps, free from denominational ambitions. He ministered to Anglicans and Dissenters in England exactly as Zinzendorf ministered to Lutherans and Reformed in Germany. The diaspora network taken over into Methodism explains Wesley's ambiguous relationship with the Church of England, not any lingering fondness for church legitimacy or apostolic succession. In his diaspora mission, moreover, he acted essentially as a layman working through other laymen, not as an ordained priest (again, like Zinzendorf in Germany). The legacy of the diaspora mission explains Methodism in the first of its essential characteristics; the legacy of the *Bußkampf* explains it in the second. This is its commitment to a distinctive kind of evangelism.

The *Bußkampf* as the first step on the way to conversion, and perfection is crucial to Methodist theology. Wesley learned about it from the Moravians and, under their direction, experienced his own conversion. He clung to the *Bußkampf* when they abandoned it. The quarrel at Fetter Lane is not between Lutheran evangelicals and Anglican sacramentalists, but between pietists of two different kinds arguing over the techniques of conversion. Once he broke with the Moravians, he persists in *Bußkampf* with stubborn tenacity: conviction precedes conversion. The *Bußkampf* accounts for the enthusiasm in the Methodist revival. It is on these two points of contact that Methodism in its defining characteristics derives from German Pietism.

Notes

CHAPTER 1

1. Daniel Benham, *Memoirs of James Hutton*, pp. 88–89; the fullest study of the Brethren's work in the formation of devotional societies is O. Steinecke, *Die Diaspora der Brüdergemeine in Deutschland;* Steinecke, who limited his work to Germany, says nothing about Fetter Lane.

2. Ibid., 1:52–53, 2:158; and J. E. Hutton, *A History of the Moravian Church,* p. 444.

3. John Wesley, *The Journal of the Rev. John Wesley, A.M. Sometime Fellow of Lincoln College, Oxford,* 1:458 (hereafter cited as *Journal*); and Charles Wesley, *The Journal of the Rev. Charles Wesley, M.A., Sometime Student of Christ Church, Oxford,* 1:137, 141, 150, 216.

4. David Cranz, *Alte und neue Brüder-Historie*, pp. 141, 154; *Kurze, zuverläßige Nachricht von der unter dem Namen der Böhmisch-Märischen Brüder bekanten Kirche Unitas Fratrum*, pp. 51–52; Hans-Joachim Wollstadt, *Geordnetes Dienen in der christlichen Gemeinde*, pp. 72–73; Gottfried Schmidt, "Die Banden oder Gesellschaften im alten Herrnhut," pp. 168–69; and August Gottlieb Spangenberg, *Apologetische Schlußschrift*, pp. 383–84.

5. Benham, *Hutton*, pp. 29–32; and John Wesley, *The Works of John Wesley*, 8:272–73; hereafter cited as *Works*.

6. Benham, *Hutton*, pp. 45–46, 53–54.

7. Wesley, *Journal*, 2:313.

8. Luke Tyerman, *The Life and Times of the Rev. John Wesley, M.A., Founder of the Methodists*, 1:271.

9. Charles Wesley, *Journal of Charles Wesley*, 1:207, 233–34, 239.

10. John Wesley, *Journal*, 2:351, 352, 363, 365, 366, 369, 370, 371.

11. John Wesley, *The Letters of the Rev. John Wesley, A.M. Sometime Fellow of Lincoln College*, 1:286; hereafter cited as *Letters*.

12. John Wesley, *Journal*, 8:231.

13. John Wesley, *Letters*, 3:194–95.

14. Ibid., pp. 150–51, 222–23.

15. Ibid., 4:216–17; and Henry D. Rack, *Reasonable Enthusiast*, pp. 286–89, 303–4.

16. John Wesley, *Letters*, 5:312, 7:163, 8:58, 143.

17. John Wesley, *Journal*, 4:11, 469, 487.

18. Tyerman, *Life and Times of Wesley*, 3:23; and John Wesley, *Letters*, 5:330.

19. John Wesley, *Works*, 8:321; and *Letters*, 8:136.

20. Tyerman, *Life and Times of Wesley*, 3:496–97, 574–76.

21. John C. Bowmer, *Pastor and People*, p. 238; and Fred M. Parkinson, "Methodist Class Tickets," pp. 133.

22. Halévy, *The Birth of Methodism in England*, pp. 5, 49–51; and Halévy, *England in 1815*, pp. 389–90, 415.

23. Thompson, *The Making of the English Working Class*, pp. 350, 362.

24. Bernard Semmel, *The Methodist Revolution*, pp. 20–21.

25. Frank Baker, *John Wesley and the Church of England*, p. 137; Bowmer, *Pastor and People*, p. 260; Michael R. Watts, *The Dissenters*, pp. 434–35, 440.

26. John Wesley, *The Works of John Wesley*, ed. Frank Baker (Oxford: Clarendon Press; Nashville: Abingdon Press, 1975–), vol. 25, *Letters I: 1721–1739*, ed. Frank Baker (1980), p. 3; and Frank Baker, "The People Called Methodists," pp. 213–14.

27. John Wesley, *Works*, 8:374; and *Letters*, 5:358.

28. Cranz, *Brüder-Historie*, pp. 252–53; Erich Beyreuther, *Zinzendorf und die Christenheit*, pp. 90–91; for the relationship between the new Moravianism of the United Brethren and the old Moravianism of the congregation that survived at Lissa in Poland, see W. Bickerich, "Lissa und Herrnhut," pp. 1–74.

29. John Wesley, *Journal*, 1:110–112, 2:496.

30. Ibid., 1:168–69, 195, 436–37.

31. Ibid., p. 151.

32. J. P. Lockwood, *Memorials of the Life of Peter Böhler, Bishop of the Church of the United Brethren*, p. 68; and John Wesley, *Journal*, 1:440, 442, 447, 454–55.

33. Lockwood, *Böhler*, pp. 77–79; and John Wesley, *Journal*, 1:460–61.

34. Philipp Jacob Spener, *Pia Desideria*, p. 34; Nikolaus Ludwig von Zinzendorf, *Sonderbare Gespräche zwischen einem Reisenden und allerhand andern Personen, von allerley in der Religion vorkommenden Wahrheiten*, p. 12; Erich Beyreuther, *August Hermann Francke, 1663–1727*, p. 54; and *Die Religion in Geschichte und Gegenwart*, 3rd ed, s.v. "Wesley."

35. John Wesley, *Journal*, 1:475–76; and Charles Wesley, *Journal of Charles Wesley*, 1:95.

36. John Wesley, *Journal*, 1:483, 2:13; and *Letters*, 1:250–51.

37. Towlson, *Moravian and Methodist*, pp. 19, 62; and Watts, *Dissenters*, p. 428.

38. John Wesley, *Journal*, 1:171; and *Works*, 8:347–451.

39. Ibid., 7:419–30.

40. Ibid., 13:307.

41. Ibid., 8:258–61.

42. Ibid., pp. 269–71.

43. Ibid., pp. 248–68.

44. Richard Green, *The Works of John and Charles Wesley*, pp. 14–16.

Chapter 2

1. Frederick Hunter, "Sources of Wesley's Revision of the Prayer Book in 1784–8," p. 129; John Wesley, *Letters*, 4:216; and *Journal* 4:64.

2. John Wesley, *Works*, 8:340.

3. Ibid., 270; and John Wesley, *Journal*, 7:389.

4. John Wesley, *Works*, 7:276–77, 13:266.

5. August Gottlieb Spangenberg, *Leben des Herrn Nikolaus Ludwig Graf von Zinzendorf und Pottendorf*, vols. 5–6, pp. 1570–73; Joseph T. Müller, *Zinzendorf als Erneurer der alten Brüderkirche*, pp. 91–95; and August Gottlieb Spangenberg, *Apologetische Schlußschrift*, p. 43.

6. Otto Uttendörfer, *Zinzendorfs Weltbetrachtung*, pp. 84–85; Spangenberg, *Apologetische Schlußschrift*, pp. 39–40; and Daniel Benham, *Memoirs of James Hutton*, pp. 243–45.

7. Müller, *Zinzendorf als Erneurer der alten Brüderkirche*, pp. 92–93; David

Cranz, *Alte und neue Brüder-Historie*, p. 485; and Spangenberg, *Leben des Herrn Graf von Zinzendorf*, vol. 5–6. pp. 1800, 1806.

8. Spangenberg, *Idea Fidei Fratrum*, p. 537.

9. Schrautenbach, *Der Graf von Zinzendorf und die Brüdergemeinde seiner Zeit*, p. 43; and Uttendörfer, *Zinzendorfs Weltbetrachung*, pp. 67–89.

10. John Wesley, *Works*, 5:78, 8:363.

11. John Wesley, *Works*, 5:85; and *Letters*, 3:222, 2:383.

12. John Newton, *Methodism and the Puritans*, pp. 7–8; and August Lang, *Puritanismus und Pietismus*, pp. 273–75, 349.

13. Philip Schaff, *The Creeds of Christendom: With a History and Critical Notes*, 3:637–40.

14. John Wesley, *Works*, ed. Baker, vol. 25, *Letters I: 1721–1739*, ed. Baker (1980), p. 179.

15. John Wesley, *Journal*, 2:267–68.

16. Spener, *Pia desideria*, pp. 27, 66; and Martin Schmidt, *Wiedergeburt und neuer Mensch*, pp. 129–68.

17. Beyreuther, *August Hermann Francke, 1663–1727*, p. 35; and Erhard Peschke, *Studien zur Theologie August Hermann Franckes*, 1:36.

18. Martin Luther, *Reformation Writings of Martin Luther*, 2:288–89.

19. Spener, *Pia desideria*, p. 34; Beyreuther, *Francke*, p. 54; *Die Religion in Geschichte und Gegenwart*, 3d ed., s.v. "Wesley."; and Schmidt, *Wiedergeburt und neuer Mensch*, pp. 299–330.

20. Schmidt, *Pietismus*, pp. 12–16.

21. Walter Wendland, "Die pietistische Bekehrung," pp. 214–15.

22. Peschke, *Studien zur Theologie August Hermann Franckes*, 1:105–6; and Martin Schmidt, *Wiedergeburt und neuer Mensch*, pp. 238–98.

23. John Wesley, *John Wesley*, ed. Albert Cook Outler, pp. 367–70.

24. Peschke, *Studien zur Theologie August Hermann Franckes*, 1:45–47, 57–58.

25. Spangenberg, *Apologetische Schlußschrift*, pp. 445, 636; *Leben des Herrn Graf von Zinzendorf*, vols. 3–4, pp. 535; and Bernhard Becker, *Zinzendorf im Verhältnis zu Philosophie und Kirchentum seiner Zeit*, pp. 178–88.

26. Otto Uttendörfer, *Das Erziehungswesen Zinzendorfs und der Brüdergemeine in seinen Anfängen*, pp. 15–17.

27. Uttendörfer, *Zinzendorfs religiöse Grundgedanken*, p. 37; and Gottfried Schmidt, "Die Banden oder Gesellschaften im alten Herrnhut," p. 151.

28. Spangenberg, *Leben des Herrn Graf von Zinzendorf*, vols. 3–4, pp. 671–72; and John Wesley, *Journal*, 2:54; Wesley quotes from a copy of the Herrnhut constitution, dated 1733. Whether he actually witnessed band selection with his own eyes, is not certain.

29. Schmidt, "Die Banden oder Gesellschaften," pp. 151, 160–61.

30. Cranz, *Brüder-Historie*, p. 230; and Spangenberg, *Leben des Herrn Graf von Zinzendorf*, vols. 3–4, pp. 408–9; and Schrautenbach, *Zinzendorf*, pp. 47, 223–24.

31. Spangenberg, *Leben des Herrn Graf von Zinzendorf*, vols. 5–6:1284; and Schrautenbach, *Zinzendorf*, p. 225.

32. Spangenberg, *Apologetische Schlußschrift*, pp. 27–28, 244.

33. Ibid., 621–22.

34. Ibid., p. 247; and Nikolaus Ludwig von Zinzendorf, *Des Ordinarii Fratrum Berlinische Reden*, pp. 29–30.

35. Albrecht Ritschl, *Geschichte des Pietismus*, 2:252–53, 257–58; and Spangenberg, *Apologetische Schlußschrift*, p. 241.

36. Nikolaus Ludwig Zinzendorf, ed., *Büdingische Sammlung einiger in die Kirchen-Historie einschlagender sonderlich neuerer Schriften*, vol. 7, p. 156;

Spangenberg, *Apologetische Schlußschrift*, p. 241; and *Idea Fidei Fratrum*, pp. 247, 162, 165–66.

37. Cranz, *Brüder-Historie*, p. 231; and Schrautenbach, *Zinzendorf*, p. 225.

38. Otto Uttendörfer, *Zinzendorf und die Mystik*, pp. 143–47.

39. Uttendörfer, *Das Erziehungswesen Zinzendorfs und der Brüdergemeine*, pp. 229–31; John Taylor Hamilton, *History of the Church known as the Moravian Church, or the Unitas Fratrum, or the Unity of the Brethren, during the Eighteenth and Nineteenth Centuries*, pp. 190–92; and Spangenberg, *Leben des Herrn Graf von Zinzendorf*, vols. 5–6, pp. 1283–84.

40. Zinzendorf, ed., *Büdingsche Sammlung*, vol. 7, p. 622; and John Holmes, *Historical Sketches of the Missions of the United Brethren for Propagating the Gospel among the Heathen from their Commencement to the Year 1817*, p. 24.

41. Holmes, *Historical Sketches*, pp. 30–31; and Uttendörfer, *Zinzendorf und die Mystik*, p. 163.

42. Zinzendorf, ed., *Büdingsche Sammlung*, vol. 8, p. 138.

43. Spangenberg, *Leben des Herrn Graf von Zinzendorf*, vols. 3–4, p. 491; and Gerhard Reichel, *August Gottlieb Spangenberg: Bischof der Brüderkirche*, pp. 123, 136.

44. John Wesley, *Journal*, 1:151, 372–73; and *Letters*, 5:281.

45. Martin Schmidt, *John Wesley: Leben und Werk*, 1:142; and John Wesley, *Journal*, 1:461–62.

46. John Wesley, *The Works of John Wesley*, ed. Frank Baker and Richard P. Heitzenrater (Oxford: Clarendon Press; Nashville: Abingdon Press, 1975–), vol. 18, *Journals and Diaries I: 1735–38*, ed. Reginald W. Ward and Richard P. Heitzenrater (1988), pp. 355, 361, 365, 384, 387.

47. Ibid., 369, 379, 384.

48. John Wesley, *Journal*, 1:193.

49. John Wesley, *Works*, ed. Baker and Heitzenrater, vol. 18, *Journal and Diaries I: 1735–38*, ed. Ward and Heitzenrater (1988), pp. 317, 382, 383, 426–427.

50. Ibid., 375, 529.

51. John Wesley, *Journal*, 1:415–16, 417, 422–24, 470–71.

52. Ibid., 2:26–27, 36.

53. Ibid., 2:71–72, 278–79.

54. Charles Wesley, *Journal*, 1:168, 186; and John Wesley, *Works*, ed. Baker and Heitzenrater, vol. 18, *Journals and Diaries I: 1735–38*, ed. Ward and Heitzenrater (1988), pp. 354, 383, 384, 386, 387, 389, 390, 392, 394, 401.

55. Benham, *Hutton*, p. 53.

56. Otto Uttendörfer, "Zinzendorf und die Entwicklung des theologischen Seminars der Brüderunität," p. 77; and Hans-Walther Erbe, *Zinzendorf und der fromme hohe Adel seiner Zeit*, pp. 561–74.

57. Georg Loskiel, *Geschichte der Mission der evangelische Brüder unter den Indianern in Nordamerika*, pp. 212–13.

58. Spangenberg, *Apologetische Schlußschrift*, p. 290; and [A.] Loebich, "Zinzendorf und der Pietismus seiner Zeit," pp. 159–60.

59. Spangenberg, *Apologetische Schlußschrift*, p. 109; Benham, *Hutton*, pp. 10, 113; and Uttendörfer, *Zinzendorfs Weltbetrachtung*, p. 85.

60. Uttendörfer, *Zinzendorfs religiöse Grundgedanken*, p. 81.

61. John Wesley, *Works*, 10:201; and Tyerman, *Wesley*, 2:467.

62. Baumgarten, *Von den so genannten Herrnhutern oder mährischen Brüdergemeinen*, pp. 156–60; Lange, *Väterliche Warnung an die der Theologie studierende Jugend*, pp. 260–61; and Walch, *Theologisches Bedencken von der Beschaffenheit*

der Herrnhutischen Secte, und wie sich ein Landes-Herr in Ansehung derselbigen zu verhalten habe, pp. 48–49.

63. John Wesley, *Works,* 8:269–71.
64. Ibid.
65. John Wesley, *Letters,* 1:280–81; and *Works,* 8: 130–31.
66. John Wesley, *Letters,* 5:366–67.
67. John Wesley, *Journal,* 4:480.
68. John Wesley, *Works,* 5:81–84.
69. Ibid., p. 104.
70. John Wesley, *Letters,* 5:104.
71. John Wesley, *Works,* 7:199–200.
72. Ibid., p. 236.

Chapter 3

1. Arnold A. Dallimore, *George Whitefield,* 1:72–77.
2. Hervey, *The Whole Works of the Rev. James Hervey, A.M.,* 3:14.
3. Gordon Rupp, *Religion in England, 1688–1791,* pp. 476–78; and G. R. Balleine, *A History of the Evangelical Party in the Church of England,* pp. 81, 131–33.
4. John C. Bowmer, *Pastor and People,* pp. 173–74; and Frank Baker, "People Called Methodists," pp. 223–24.
5. John Wesley, *Letters,* 2:239.
6. John Wesley, *Works,* 8:269.
7. Baker, "People Called Methodists," pp. 222–24; Bowmer, *Pastor and People,* pp. 173–76; and Gottfried Schmidt, "Die Banden oder Gesellschaften im alten Herrnhut," pp. 145–207.
8. David Lowes Watson, "The Origins and Significance of the Early Methodist Class Meeting," pp. 400–2; and John Wesley, *Works,* 8:301.
9. John Wesley, *Letters,* 8:196; and *Works,* 13:516.
10. John S. Simon, "John Wesley's 'Deed of Declaration'," pp. 81–82; and E. Benson Perkins, *Methodist Preaching Houses and the Law,* pp. 18–22, 31–38; and John Wesley, *Journal,* 8:335–41.
11. Bowmer, *Pastor and People,* pp. 190–91.
12. John Wesley, *Works,* 8:311–13.
13. Ibid.
14. Baker, "People Called Methodists," p. 213; and Henry D. Rack, *Reasonable Enthusiast,* pp. 237–38.
15. John Wesley, *Letters,* 2:292.
16. Ibid., pp. 292, 293–94, 296–97, 301, 303, 304.
17. John Wesley, *Works,* 8:220.
18. H. Bauer, "Das Diasporawerk der Brüdergemeine," pp. 149–57; and Bernhard Becker, *Zinzendorf im Verhältnis zu Philosophie und Kirchentum seiner Zeit,* pp. 507–14.
19. O. Steinecke, *Die Diaspora der Brüdergemeine in Deutschland,* 1:4; and Bauer, "Das Diasporawerk der Brüdergemeine," p. 167.
20. Otto Uttendörfer, "Zinzendorf und die Entwicklung des theologischen Seminars der Brüderunität," pp. 44–47; and Gerhard Reichel, *August Gottlieb Spangenberg: Bischof der Brüderkirche,* pp. 55–57.
21. Steinecke, *Diaspora der Brüdergemeine,* 1:66; and Gerhard Meyer, *Gnadefrei,* pp. 52–62.
22. W. Bickerich, "Lissa und Herrnhut," pp. 20–26.

23. Ibid., pp. 10–13, 26–29.

24. R. Geiges, "Johann Conrad Lange und die Anfänge der herrnhutischen Gemeinschaftspflege in Württemberg," pp. 9–12; and Steinecke, *Diaspora der Brüdergemeine*, 1:52.

25. Geiges, "Lange," pp. 11, 32, 45, 46; and Steinecke, *Diaspora der Brüdergemeine*, 1:49–52.

26. Steinecke, *Diaspora der Brüdergemeine*, 2:106–7.

27. Geiges, "Lange," pp. 21–22; and Cranz, *Alte und neue Brüder-Historie*, pp. 397–98, 620–21.

28. Steinecke, *Diaspora der Brüdergemeine*, 2:183–88.

29. Ibid., 2:102–5, 3:5.

30. Cranz, *Alte und neue Brüder-Historie*, p. 639; and H. Steinberg, *Hundert Jahre im Ringgäßlein, 1811–1911*, pp. 47–59.

31. August Gottlieb Spangenberg, *Leben des Herrn Nikolaus Ludwig Graf von Zinzendorf und Pottendorf*, vols., 5–6, pp. 1473–74; Zinzendorf, *Die gegenwärtige Gestalt des Kreuz-Reichs Jesu in seiner Unschuld*, p. 5; and Benham, *James Hutton*, p. 129.

32. Hans-Joachim Wollstadt, *Geordnetes Dienen in der christlichen Gemeinde*, pp. 147–48; to learn how Herrnhut actually worked as a system of civil and ecclesiastical administration, see Otto Uttendörfer, *Alt-Herrnhut: Wirtschaftsgeschichte und Religionssoziologie Herrnhuts während seiner ersten zwanzig Jarhe (1722–1742)*.

33. Schrautenbach, *Der Graf von Zinzendorf und die Brüdergemeinde seiner Zeit*, p. 274; Spangenberg, *Leben des Herrn Graf von Zinzendorf*, vols. 3–4, pp. 508–9; Spangenberg, *Apologetische Schlußschrift*, pp. 501–2; and Steinecke, *Diaspora der Brüdergemeine*, 1:56–57, 3:12–13.

34. Uttendörfer, *Alt-Herrnhut*, pp. 19–45.

35. Gottfried Schmidt, "Die Banden oder Gesellschaften im alten Herrnhut," pp. 182–89; and John Wesley, *Journal*, 1:459.

36. Benham, *Hutton*, pp. 130–33; and Schmidt, "Die Banden oder Gesellschaften im alten Herrnhut," pp. 196–99.

37. John Wesley, *Journal*, 1:195–205, 226–32. On his first Sunday in Georgia, we know that Spangenberg attended the Anglican service. See Adelaide Fries, *The Moravians in Georgia: 1735–1740*, p. 68, and for the institution of a Moravian society in Georgia, p. 129.

38. John Wesley, *Journal*, 1:436–38; Charles Wesley, *Journal of Charles Wesley*, 1:131; and Schmidt, "Banden oder Gesellschaften im alten Herrnhut," pp. 183–84.

39. John Wesley, *Journal*, 2:3–7; and *Letters*, 1:250.

40. John Wesley, *Journal*, 2:16, 22, 56, 60.

41. John Wesley, *Letters*, 1:250–51; and *Journal*, 2:28.

42. John Wesley, *Journal*, 2:70–131; and *Letters*, 1:260.

43. John Wesley, *Letters*, 1:280, 283–84; and *Journal*, 2:146.

44. John Wesley, *Works*, ed. Baker, (Oxford: Clarendon Press; Nashville: Abingdon Press, 1975–), vol. 25, *Letters I, 1721–1739*, ed. Baker (1980), pp. 605–9, 610–12.

45. John Wesley, *Journal*, 2:158, 172, 174–75.

46. Steinecke, *Diaspora der Brüdergemeine*, 3:5, 12–13; and Steinberg, *Hundert Jahre in Ringgäßlein*, pp. 60–64.

47. For recent statements of the argument that Methodism derives from the Anglican society-movement, see John Walsh, "Religious Societies: Methodist and Evangelical, 1738–1800," pp. 279–302; David Pike, "The Religious Societies, 1678–1738," pp. 15–20, 32–38; and Henry D. Rack, "Religious Societies and the Origins of Methodism," pp. 582–95.

48. Geiges, "Lange," pp. 20–21; and Steinecke, *Diaspora der Brüdergemeine,* 3:45–46.

49. Spangenberg, *Leben des Herrn Graf von Zinzendorf,* vols. 3–4, pp. 484, 1045–47; Cranz, *Alte und neue Brüder-Historie,* 249–50; Charles Wesley, *Journal,* 1:65–66; Schmidt, "Die Banden oder Gesellschaften im alten Herrnhut," pp. 183–84; and John Wesley, *Journal,* 1:436–37.

50. John Wesley, *Works,* ed. Baker, vol. 25, *Letters I: 1721–1739,* ed. Baker, pp. 615–16; and Uttendörfer, *Zinzendorf und die Mystik,* p. 165.

51. Richard Green, *The Works of John and Charles Wesley: A Bibliography,* pp. 139, 180; and Luke Tyerman, *The Life and Times of the Rev. John Wesley,* 3:186.

52. Green, *Works of John and Charles Wesley,* pp. 157–58, 162–65, 172–74.

53. Ibid., p. 62; and John Wesley, ed., *A Christian Library: Consisting of Extracts and Abridgements of the Choicest Pieces of Practical Divinity which have been Published in the English Tongue,* 30 vols. (London: J. Kershaw, 1827).

54. Green, *Works of John and Charles Wesley,* p. 125.

55. John Wesley, *Explanatory Notes upon the New Testament,* 1: unpag. preface.

56. John Wesley, *Letters,* 2:311.

CHAPTER 4

1. Peter Gay, *The Enlightenment,* p. 254.

2. Ibid.

3. Stephen, *History of English Thought in the Eighteenth Century,* 2:369.

4. Schmidt, *John Wesley: Leben und Werk,* 3:43, 49–50, 181–83.

5. Erich Beyreuther, *Zinzendorf und Pierre Bayle,* p. 7.

6. V. H. H. Green, *The Young Mr. Wesley: A Study of John Wesley and Oxford,* pp. 305–19; and John Wesley, *Journal,* 4:190, 5:247.

7. John Wesley, *Journal,* 4:53–54; Green, *Works of John and Charles Wesley: A Bibliography,* pp. 114–15; and John Wesley, *Works,* 14:241.

8. Wesley, *Journal,* 6:63; Nikolaus Ludwig von Zinzendorf, *Der teutsche Sokrates,* unpag. pref.; and Otto Uttendörfer, *Zinzendorfs religiöse Grundgedanken,* p. 11.

9. Walther Wendland, "Die pietistische Bekehrung," pp. 193–238; and Hans R. G. Günther, "Psychologie des deutschen Pietismus," pp. 144–76.

10. John Wesley, *Journal,* 1:415, 2:125–26.

11. John Wesley, *Journal,* 1:476; and *Letters,* 2:64.

12. Spangenberg, *Apologetische Schlußschrift,* pp. 25–26, 129, 629.

13. Zinzendorf, *Der teutsche Sokrates,* unpag. intro.; and Leiv Aalen, *Die Theologie des jungen Zinzendorf,* pp. 108–9, 115–16, 149–53; Thomasius is better remembered for jurisprudence than for metaphysics. For the latter, see his *Einleitung zur Vernunftlehre* (1691); and for a discussion of his status as an empiricist, see Rita Widmaier, "Alter und neuer Empirismus. Zur Erfahrungslehre von Locke und Thomasius," pp. 95–114.

14. Spangenberg, *Leben des Herrn Nikolaus Ludwig Graf von Zinzendorf und Pottendorf,* vols. 1–2, pp. 380–81; and Bernhard Becker, *Zinzendorf im Verhältnis zu Philosophie und Kirchentum seiner Zeit,* pp. 37–38.

15. V. H. H. Green, *The Young Mr. Wesley,* pp. 191, 315; John Wesley, *Letters,* 4:249, 7:82, 228; and John Wesley, ed., *The Arminian Magazine,* 5 (London, 1782): 27–648, ibid., 6 (1783): 30–652, and ibid., 7 (1784): 32–302.

16. John Wesley, *Works,* 7:231, 8:13, 13:464.

17. John Wesley, *Journal,* 5:265; and *Works,* 6:204, 14:310–11.

18. John Wesley, *Journal*, 5:266, 311; and *Works*, 14:301.

19. John Wesley, *Works*, 13:454–55; and *Letters*, 6:229.

20. Browne, *The Procedure, Extent, and Limits of Human Understanding*, pp. 63–69, 412–14.

21. Ibid., 205–9.

22. John Wesley, *Letters*, 1:56–58, 3:163, 4:249.

23. Browne, *Limits of Human Understanding*, p. 51; and John Wesley, *Journal*, 4:192.

24. Erich Beyreuther, *Studien zur Theologie Zinzendorfs*, p. 220; and Uttendörfer, *Zinzendorfs religiöse Grundgedanken*, p. 10.

25. Zinzendorf, *Der teutsche Sokrates*, pp. 289–90.

26. John Wesley, *Letters*, 3:104–5, 8:89.

27. Browne, *Limits of Human Understanding*, pp. 290–302, 473–77; and John Wesley, *Works*, 6:204.

28. Nikolaus Ludwig von Zinzendorf, *Sieben letzte Reden*, pp. 6–7; and Beyreuther, *Studien*, p. 21.

29. Beyreuther, *Studien*, p. 12; Uttendörfer, *Zinzendorfs religiöse Grundgedanken*, p. 57; and Zinzendorf, *Sieben letze Reden*, p. 6.

30. Beyreuther, *Studien*, pp. 20, 25; Zinzendorf, *Sieben letzte Reden*, p. 4; and Uttendörfer, *Zinzendorfs religiöse Grundgedanke*, p. 53.

31. Uttendörfer, *Zinzendorfs religiöse Grundgedanken*, pp. 53, 65–66.

32. Betterman, *Theologie und Sprache bei Zinzendorf*, pp. 20, 72.

33. John Wesley, *Journal*, 1:465, 471, 2:251, 6:18; *Letters*, 1:245, 329–30, 3:160, 4:35, 231, 5:8, 363; and *Works*, 5:115, 117, 120.

34. John Wesley, *Journal*, 6:18; *Letters*, 1:245, 329, 2:64, 206, 4:35, 331, 5:363, 364; and *Works*, 5:78–79, 8:106, 276.

35. John Wesley, *Letters*, 1:329–30, 4:35.

36. Ibid., 1:20, 2:64, 4:332.

37. Ibid., 5:363; John Wesley, *Journal* 2:125; and *Works*, 5:114.

38. John Wesley, *Works*, 5:115, 128–29; and *Letters*, 5:8, 21–22.

39. John Wesley, *Works*, 6:47; and *Letters*, 2:92, 4:176.

40. John Wesley, *Works*, 8:13–14.

41. Ibid., 5:224–27.

42. Ibid., 5:121–22, 8:46; and John Wesley, *Letters*, 3:174, 235.

43. John Wesley, *Journal*, 4:425; *Letters*, 3:159; and *Works*, 9:168–70.

44. John Wesley, *Journal*, 5:458.

45. Hume, *Philosophical Works*, 1:475.

46. John Wesley, *Works*, 8:5–6.

47. Hume, *Philosophical Works*, 1:555, 4:41.

48. Ibid., 1:385.

49. John Wesley, *Works*, 5:121–22.

50. Hume, *Philosophical Works*, 1:398, 4:41.

51. Locke, *An Essay Concerning Human Understanding*, 1:6, 2:281; and Browne, *Limits of Human Understanding*. 240, 247–56.

52. John Wesley, *Works*, 7:189, 13:467.

53. Ibid., 5:135–36.

54. Otto Uttendörfer, *Zinzendorf und die Mystik*, p. 16; Zinzendorf, ed., *Büdingsche Sammlung einiger in die Kirchen-Historie einschlagender sonderlich neuerer Schriften*, vol. 8, pp. 8–10; and Beyreuther, *Die Bedeutung der tschechischen Exulantengemeinde Nakopecku im Nachbarort Herrnhuts 1724–1734*, pp. 785–94.

55. Becker, *Zinzendorf im Verhältnis zu Philosophie und Kirchentum*, pp. 111–12; Spangenberg, *Idea Fidei Fratrum*, p. 540.

56. Cranz, *Alte und neue Brüder-Historie*, pp. 139–40; Joseph T. Müller, *Zinzendorf als Erneurer der alten Brüderkirche*, pp. 29–31; and Joachim Wollstadt, *Geordnetes Dienen in der christlichen Gemeinde*, pp. 38–39.

57. J. E. Hutton, *A History of the Moravian Church*, p. 443; and Loskiel, *Geschichte der Mission der evangelische Brüder unter den Indianern in Nordamerika*, pp. 369–70.

58. Benham, *Memoirs of James Hutton*, pp. 237–40; and John Wesley, *Journal*, 1:170–71.

59. Zinzendorf, *Büdingsche Sammlung*, vol. 7, p. 164; and Hutton, *History of Moravian Missions*, p. 130.

60. Spangenberg, *Declaration über die zeither gegen uns ausgegange Beschuldigungen*, p. 44; *Apologetische Schlußschrift*, pp. 21–22; *Leben des Herrn Graf von Zinzendorf*, vols. 3–4, pp. 893–96; in 1736, Zinzendorf sent an ordained minister to Georgia to avoid giving offense to other denominations, "although our Brethren in other Colonies are served by laymen, as permitted by our ancient constitution"; Fries, *Moravians in Georgia*, pp. 71–72.

61. John Wesley, *Journal*, 1:169; and *Letters*, 1:349–50.

62. John Wesley, *Journal*, 2:307–11, 490–95.

63. John Wesley, *Journal*, 3:232; and *Letters*, 3:182.

64. John Wesley, *Works*, 8:30–31; Baker, "John Wesley's Churchmanship," p. 214; and John Wesley, *Letters*, 3:332.

65. John Wesley, *Letters*, 2:233–34; and *Works*, 6:397.

66. John Wesley, *Letters*, 2:293; *Works*, 5:78, 6:199, 397; and *Journal*, 5:244.

67. Geoffrey Nuttall, *Visible Saints*, pp. 111–15, 131–32; and John Wesley, *Letters*, 4:273.

68. John Wesley, *Letters*, 3:9; and *Works*, 6:400.

69. John Wesley, *Letters*, 3:35; *Journal*, 2:361–62; and *Works*, 7:184.

70. John Wesley, *Works*, 5:491; *Letters*, 4:333; and *Journal*, 4:415.

71. John Wesley, *Letters*, 5:17; *Journal*, 4:536; and *Works*, 11:428.

72. T. G. Crippen, ed., "The Covenant and Confession of Faith of the Church of Christ, Meeting in Blanket-Row, Kingston-upon-Hull," p. 253; Nuttall, *Visible Saints*, pp. 71–80; and Horton Davies, *Worship and Theology in England from Watts and Wesley to Maurice, 1690–1850*, pp. 196–99; and John Wesley, *Letters*, 2:298, 302.

73. John Wesley, *Letters*, 2:239.

74. Ibid., 3:188; Luke Tyerman, *Life and Times of the Rev. John Wesley, M.A., Founder of the Methodists*, 3:496–98, 574–76; and John Wesley, *Works*, 7:277.

75. John Wesley, *Works*, 5:77–78, 497, 499, 10:113; and *Letters*, 3:36.

76. John Wesley, *Works*, 6:73–74.

77. John Wesley, *Journal* 2:212, 3:494; *Works*, 5:488; and *Letters*, 3:186.

78. John Wesley, *Works*, 7:65; and John Wesley, *The Works of John Wesley*, ed. Baker, vol. 26, *Letters II: 1740–1755*, ed. Baker (1980): 419.

79. John Wesley, *Works*, 7:424; *Journal*, 1:275, 419–20, 4:97; and *Letters*, 2:387.

80. John Wesley, *Works*, 14:223; and *Journal*, 3:243.

81. John Wesley, *Works*, 11:37–38; and John Wesley, *Minutes of the Methodist Conferences, from the First Held in London by the Late Rev. John Wesley A.M., in the Year 1744*, pp. 27–28.

CHAPTER 5

1. John Wesley, *Works*, 7:236.

2. John Wesley, *Journal*, 1:430–31.

3. John Wesley, *The Works of John Wesley,* ed. Baker, vol. 26, *Letters II: 1740–1755,* ed Baker (1980): 419, 423, 424–26.

4. Thompson, *Making of the English Working Class,* pp. 355–56, 365, 379–80.

5. J. C. D. Clark, *English Society, 1688–1832,* pp. 235–36.

6. Semmel, *Methodist Revolution.*

Bibliography

Aalen, Leiv. *Die Theologie des jungen Zinzendorf.* Berlin: Lutherisches Verlagshaus, 1966.

Baker, Frank. *John Wesley and the Church of England.* London: Epworth Press, 1970.

————. "John Wesley's Churchmanship." *London Quarterly and Holborn Review* 6th ser. 29 (1960):210–15, 269–74.

————. "The People Called Methodists—3. Polity." In *A History of the Methodist Church in Great Britain.* Rupert Davies and Gordon Rupp, eds., pp. 211–57. London: Epworth Press, 1965.

Balleine, G. R. *A History of the Evangelical Party in the Church of England.* London: Longmans, Green, and Co., 1909.

Bauer, H. "Das Diasporawerk der Brüdergemeine." *Zeitschrift für Brüdergeschichte.* 1911. In Nikolaus Ludwig von Zinzendorf: Materialen und Dokumente. Erich Beyreuther, and Gerhard Meyer, eds., 3rd ser., vol. 2, pp. 125–87. Reprint, Hildesheim: Georg Olms Verlag, 1973.

Baumgarten, Sigmund Jakob. *Von den so genannten Herrnhutern oder mährischen Brüdergemeinen.* 1742. Reprint in Nikolaus Ludwig von Zinzendorf: Materialen und Dokumente. Erich Beyreuther, ed., 2nd ser., vol. 16. Hildesheim: Georg Olms Verlag, 1982.

Becker, Bernhard. *Zinzendorf im Verhältnis zu Philosophie und Kirchentum seiner Zeit.* Geschichtliche Studien. Leipzig: J. C. Hinrichs'sche Buchhandlung, 1886.

Benham, Daniel. *Memoirs of James Hutton; Comprising the Annals of His Life and Connection with the United Brethren.* London: Hamilton, Adams, & Co., 1856.

Betterman, Wilhelm. *Theologie und Sprache bei Zinzendorf.* Gotha: Leopold Klotz Verlag, 1935.

Beyreuther, Erich. "Die Bedeutung der tschechischen Exulantengemeinde Nakopecku im Nachbarort Herrnhuts 1724–1734." 1959. In Nikolaus Ludwig von Zinzendorf: Materialien und Dokumente. Erich Beyreuther and Gerhard Meyer, eds., 2nd ser., vol. 12, pp. 785–94. Reprint, Hildesheim: Georg Olms Verlag, 1973.

————. *Studien zur Theologie Zinzendorfs: Gesammelte Aufsätze.* Neukirchen: Neukirchener Verlag, 1962.

————. *Zinzendorf und die Christenheit.* Marburg an der Lahn: Francke-Buchhandlung, 1961.

————. *Zinzendorf und Pierre Bayle: ein Beitrag zur Frage des Verhältnisses Zinzendorfs zur Aufklärung.* Herrnhuter Hefte. Hamburg: Direktion der Europäisch-Festländischen Brüder-Unität in Bad Boll, 1955.

————. *August Hermann Francke, 1663–1727: Zeuge des lebendiges Gottes.* Marburg an der Lahn: Francke-Buchhandlung, 1956.

Bickerich, W. "Lissa und Herrnhut." *Zeitschrift für Brüdergeschichte.* 1908. In Nikolaus Ludwig von Zinzendorf: Materialen und Dokumente. Erich Beyreuther, and

Gerhard Meyer, eds., 3rd ser. vol. 1, pp. 1–74. Reprint, Hildesheim: Georg Olms Verlag, 1973.

Bowmer, John C. *Pastor and People.* London: Epworth Press, 1975.

Browne, Peter. *The Procedure, Extent, and Limits of Human Understanding.* 1728. Reprint, New York: Garland Publishing, 1976.

Clark, J. C. D. *English Society, 1688–1832: Ideology, Social Structure and Political Practice during the Ancien Regime.* Cambridge: Cambridge University Press, 1985.

Cranz, David. *Alte und neue Brüder-Historie, oder kurzgefaßte Geschichte der Evangelischen Brüder-Unität in den ältern Zeiten und insonderheit in dem gegegwärtigen Jahrhundert.* 1772. In Nikolaus Ludwig von Zinzendorf: Materialien und Dokumente. Reprint, Erich Beyreuther and Gerhard Meyer, eds., 2nd ser., vol. 11. Hildesheim: Georg Olms Verlag, 1973.

Crippen, T. G., ed. "The Covenant and Confession of Faith of the Church of Christ, Meeting in Blanket-Row, Kingston-upon-Hull." *Transactions of the Congregational Historical Society* 9 (1924–26):247–54.

Dallimore, Arnold A. *George Whitefield: The Life and Times of the Great Evangelist of the Eighteenth-century Revival.* 2 vols. Westchester, IL: Cornerstone Books, 1970.

Davies, Horton. *Worship and Theology in England, from Watts and Wesley to Maurice, 1690–1850.* Princeton: Princeton University Press, 1961.

Erbe, Hans-Walther. *Zinzendorf und der fromme hohe Adel seiner Zeit."* 1928. In Nikolaus Ludwig von Zinzendorf: Materialien und Dokumente. Erich Beyreuther and Gerhard Meyer, eds., 2nd ser., vol 12. Reprint, Hildesheim: Georg Olms Verlag, 1975.

Fries, Adelaide L. *The Moravians in Georgia: 1735–1740.* Raleigh, NC: Privately printed, 1905.

Gay, Peter. *The Enlightenment: An Interpretation: The Rise of Modern Paganism.* New York: Knopf, 1966.

Geiges, R. "Johann Conrad Lange und die Anfänge der herrnhutischen Gemeinschaftspflege in Württemberg." *Zeitschrift für Brüdergeschichte.* 1913. In Nikolaus Ludwig von Zinzendorf: Materialen und Dokumente. Erich Beyreuther, and Gerhard Meyer. 2nd ser., vol. 3, pp. 1–65. Reprint, Hildesheim: Georg Olms Verlag, 1973.

Green, Richard. *The Works of John and Charles Wesley: A Bibliography.* 2nd ed, London: Methodist Publishing House, 1906.

Green, V. H. H. *The Young Mr. Wesley: A Study of John Wesley and Oxford.* London: Edward Arnold (Publishers) Ltd., 1961.

Günther, Hans R. G. "Psychologie des deutschen Pietismus." *Deutsche Vierteljahrsschrift für Literaturwissenschaft und Geistesgeschichte* 4 (1926):144–76.

Halévy, Elie. *The Birth of Methodism in England.* Bernard Semmel, trans. and ed. Chicago: University of Chicago Press, 1971.

———. *England in 1815.* E. I. Watkin and D. A. Barker, trans. Vol. 1 of *A History of the English People in the Nineteenth Century.* London: Ernest Benn Limited, 1961.

Hamilton, John Taylor. *A History of the Church Known as the Moravian Church, or the Unitas Fratrum, or the Unity of the Brethren, During the Eighteenth and Nineteenth Centuries.* 1900. Reprint, New York: AMS Press, 1971.

Heitzenrater, Richard P. *Wesley and the People Called Methodists.* Nashville: Abingdon Press, 1995.

Hervey, James. *The Whole Works of the Rev. James Hervey, A.M.*, 6 vols. London: Thomas Tegg, 1825.

Holmes, John. *Historical Sketches of the Missions of the United Brethren for Propagating the Gospel Among the Heathen from Their Commencement to the Year 1817.* 2nd ed. London: privately printed, 1827.

Hume, David. *The Philosophical Works of David Hume.* Thomas Hill Green and Thomas Hodge Grose, eds., 4 vols., 1886. Reprint, Aalen: Scientia Verlag, 1964.

Hunter, Frederick. "Sources of Wesley's Revision of the Prayer Book in 1784–8." *Proceedings of the Wesley Historical Society* 23 (1941–42):123–33.

Hutton, J. E. *A History of Moravian Missions.* London: Moravian Publication Office, 1922.

————. *A History of the Moravian Church.* 2nd ed. London: Moravian Publication Office, 1909.

Kurze, zuverläßige Nachricht von der unter dem Namen der Böhmisch-Märischen Brüder bekanten Kirche Unitas Fratrum, Herkommen, Lehrbegrif, äussern und innern Kirchen-Verfassung und Gebräuchen.... 1757. In Nikolaus Ludwig von Zinzendorf: Ergänzungsbände zu den Hauptschriften. Erich Beyreuther and Gerhard Meyer, eds., vol. 6. Reprint, Hildesheim: Georg Olms Verlag, 1965.

Lang, August. *Puritanismus und Pietismus: Studien zu ihrer Entwicklung von M. Butzer bis zum Methodismus.* 1941. Reprint, Darmstadt: Wissenschaftliche Buchgesellschaft, 1972.

Lange, Joachim. *Väterliche Warnung an die der Theologie studierende Jugend.* 1744. In Nikolaus Ludwig von Zinzendorf: Materialism und Dokumente, Erich Beyreuther and Gerhard Meyer, eds. 2nd ser., vol. 16. Reprint, Hildesheim: Georg Olms Verlag, 1982.

Locke, John. *An Essay Concerning Human Understanding.* John W. Yolton, ed. and intro., 2 vols. London: J. M. Dent & Sons, Everyman's Library, 1961.

Lockwood, J. P. *Memorials of the Life of Peter Böhler, Bishop of the Church of the United Brethren.* London: Wesleyan Conference Office, 1868.

Loebich, [A.]. "Zinzendorf und der Pietismus seiner Zeit." *Zeitschrift für Brüdergeschichte* 1913. In Nikolaus Ludwig von Zinzendorf: Materialen und Dokumente. Erich Beyreuther and Gerhard Meyer, eds., 3rd ser., vol. 3, pp. 129–70. Reprint, Hildesheim: Georg Olms Verlag, 1973.

Loskiel, Georg Heinrich. *Geschichte der Mission der evangelische Brüder unter den Indianern in Nordamerika.* 1789. In Nikolaus Ludwig von Zinzendorf: Materialien und Dokumente. Erich Beyreuther and Gerhard Meyer, eds., 2nd ser., vol. 21. Reprint, Hildesheim: Georg Olms Verlag, 1989.

Luther, Martin. *Reformation Writings of Martin Luther.* Bertram Lee Woolf, trans. and ed., 2 vols. London, Lutterworth Press, 1953.

Meyer, Gerhard. *Gnadefrei: eine Herrnhuter Siedlung des schlesischen Pietismus im 18. Jahrhundert.* 1943. In Nikolaus Ludwig von Zinzendorf: Materialien und Dokumente. Erich Beyreuther and Gerhard Meyer, eds., 2nd ser., vol. 22. Reprint, Hildesheim: Georg Olms Verlag, 1984.

Müller, J. T. *Zinzendorf als Erneurer der alten Brüderkirche.* 1900. In Nikolaus Ludwig von Zinzendorf: Materialien und Dokumente. Erich Beyreuther and Gerhard Meyer, eds., 2nd ser., vol. 12. Reprint, Hildesheim: Georg Olms Verlag, 1975.

Newton, John. *Methodism and the Puritans.* London: Dr. William's Trust, 1964.

Nuttall, Geoffrey F. *Visible Saints: The Congregational Way, 1640–1660.* Oxford: Basil Blackwell, 1957.

Outler, Albert Cook, ed. *John Wesley.* A Library of Protestant Thought. Oxford: Oxford University Press, 1964.

Parkinson, Fred M. "Methodist Class Tickets." *Proceedings of the Wesley Historical Society* 1 (1898):129–35.

Perkins, E. Benson. *Methodist Preaching Houses and the Law.* London: Epworth Press, 1952.

Peschke, Erhard. *Studien zur Theologie August Hermann Franckes.* 2 vols. Berlin: Evangelische Verlagsanstalt, 1964–66.

Piette, Maximin. *John Wesley in the Evolution of Protestantism.* J. B. Howard, trans. London; Sheed & Ward, 1938.

Podmore, C. J. "The Fetter Lane Society, 1738." *Proceedings of the Wesley Historical Society* 46 (1988):125–53.

———. "The Fetter Lane Society, 1739–1740." *Proceedings of the Wesley Historical Society* 47 (1990):156–86.

Pike, David. "The Religious Societies, 1768–1738." *Proceedings of the Wesley Historical Society* 35 (1965–66):15–20, 32–38.

Rack, Henry D. *Reasonable Enthusiast: John Wesley and the Rise of Methodism.* London: Epworth Press, 1989.

———. "Religious Societies and the Origins of Methodism." *Journal of Ecclesiastical History* 38 (1987):582–95.

Reichel, Gerhard. *August Gottleib Spangenberg: Bischof der Brüderkirche.* 1906. In Nikolaus Ludwig von Zinzendorf: Materialien und Dokumente. Erich Beyreuther and Gerhard Meyer, eds., 2nd ser., vol. 12. Reprint, Hildesheim: Georg Olms Verlag, 1975.

Ritschl, Albrecht. *Geschichte des Pietismus.* 3 vols. 1905. Reprint, Berlin: W. de Gruyter, 1966.

Rupp, Gordon. *Religion in England, 1688–1791.* Oxford History of the Christian Church. Oxford: Clarendon Press, 1986.

Schaff, Philip. *The Creeds of Christendom: With a History and Critical Notes.* 6th rev. ed. 3 vols. Grand Rapids, MI: Baker Book House, 1990.

Schmidt, Gottfried. "Die Banden oder Gesellschaften im alten Herrnhut." *Zeitschrift für Brüdergeschichte.* 1909. In Nikolaus Ludwig von Zinzendorf: Materialen und Dokumente. Erich Beyreuther and Gerhard Meyer, eds., 3rd ser., vol. 1, pp. 145–207. Reprint, Hildesheim: Georg Olms Verlag, 1973.

Schmidt, Martin. *John Wesley: Leben und Werk.* 2nd ed., 3 vols. Zürich: Gotthelf Verlag, 1987–88.

———. *Pietismus.* 3rd ed. Stuttgart: W. Kohlhammer, 1983.

———. *Wiedergeburt und neuer Mensch: gesammelte Studien zur Geschichte des Pietismus.* Witten: Luther Verlag, 1969.

Schrautenbach, Ludwig Carl von. *Der Graf von Zinzendorf und die Brüdergemeinde seiner Zeit.* 1851. In Nikolaus Ludwig von Zinzendorf: Materialen und Dokumente. Erich Beyreuther and Gerhard Meyer, eds., 2nd ser., vol. 9. Reprint, Hildesheim: Georg Olms Verlag, 1972.

Semmel, Bernard. *The Methodist Revolution.* New York: Basic Books, 1973.

Simon, John S. "John Wesley's 'Deed of Declaration'." *Proceedings of the Wesley Historical Society* 12 (1919):81–92.

Spangenberg, August Gottlieb. *Apologetische Schlußschrift, worin über tausend Beschuldigung gegen die Brüder-Gemeinen und ihren zeitherigen Ordinarium nach der Wahrhiet beantwortet werden. Nebst Register.* 1752. In Nikolaus Ludwig von Zinzendorf: Ergänzungsbände zu den Hauptschriften. Erich Beyreuther and Gerhard Meyer, eds., vol. 3. Reprint, Hildesheim: Georg Olms Verlag, 1964.

————. *Declaration über die zeither gegen uns ausgegange Beschuldigungen, sonderlich die Person unsers Ordinarii betreffend....* 1751. In Nikolaus Ludwig von Zinzendorf: Ergänzungsbände zu den Hauptschriften. Erich Beyreuther and Gerhard Meyer, eds., vol. 5. Reprint, Hildesheim: Georg Olms Verlag, 1965.

————. *Idea Fidei Fratrum oder kurzer Begrif der Christlichen Lehre in den evangelischen Brüdergemeinen.* Barby: Christian Friedrich Laur, 1782.

————. *Leben des Herrn Nikolaus Ludwig Graf von Zinzendorf und Pottendorf.* 1773–75. In Nikolaus Ludwig von Zinzendorf: Materialien und Dokumente. Erich Beyreuther and Gerhard Meyer, eds., 2nd ser., vols. 1–8 (8 vols. in 4). Reprint, Hildesheim: Georg Olms Verlag, 1971.

Spener, Philipp Jacob. *Pia Desideria.* Edited by Kurt Aland. 3rd ed. Kleine Texte für Vorlesungen und Übungen. Berlin: Verlag Walter de Gruyter & Co., 1964.

Steinberg, Hermann. *Hundert Jahre im Ringgäßlein, 1811–1911: Zwanglose Bilder aus der Geschichte und dem Leben der Brüder-Sozietät in Basel.* Basel: Verlag der Brüder-Sozietät, 1911.

Steinecke, O. *Die Diaspora der Brüdergemeine in Deutschland: ein Beitrag zu der Geschichte der evangelischen Kirche Deutschlands.* 3 vols. Halle: Richard Mühlmanns Verlagsbuchhandlung, 1905–11.

Stephen, Leslie. *History of English Thought in the Eighteenth Century.* 2 vols. London: Rupert Hart-Davis, 1962.

Stoeffler, F. Ernest. "Pietism, the Wesleys, and Methodist Beginnings in America" in *Continental Pietism and Early American Christianity.* F. Ernest Stoeffler, ed., pp. 184–221. Grand Rapids, MI: 1976.

————. *The Rise of Evangelical Pietism.* Leiden: E. J. Brill, 1965.

————. *German Pietism during the Eighteenth Century.* Leiden: E. J. Brill, 1973.

Thomasius, Christian. *Einleitung zur Vernunftlehre.* 1691. Reprint, Hildesheim: Georg Olms Verlag, 1968.

Thompson, E. P. *The Making of the English Working Class.* New York: Random House, Vintage, 1966.

Towlson, Clifford W. *Moravian and Methodist: Relationships and Influences in the Eighteenth Century.* London: Epworth Press, 1957.

Tyerman, Luke. *The Life and Times of the Rev. John Wesley, M.A., Founder of the Methodists.* 3 vols. New York: Harper & Brothers, 1872.

Uttendörfer, O. *Zinzendorfs Religiöse Grundgedanken.* Herrnhut: Verlag der Missionsbuchhandlung, 1935.

————. *Alt-Herrnhut: Wirtschaftsgeschichte und Religionssoziologie Herrnhuts während seiner ersten zwanzig Jarhe (1722–1742).* 1925. In Nikolaus Ludwig von Zinzendorf: Materialen und Dokumente. Erich Beyreuther and Gerhard Meyer, eds., 2nd ser., vol. 22. Reprint, Hildesheim: Georg Olms Verlag, 1984.

————. *Das Erziehungswesen Zinzendorfs und der Brüdergemeine in seinen Anfängen.* Monumenta Germaniae Paedagogica. Berlin: Weidmannsche Buchhandlung, 1912.

————. *Zinzendorfs Weltbetrachtung: eine systematische Darstellung der Gedankenwelt des Begründers der Brüdergemeine.* Berlin: Furche-Verlag, 1929.

————. "Zinzendorf und die Entwicklung des theologischen Seminars der Brüderunität." *Zeitschrift für Brüdergeschichte.* 1916. In Nikolaus Ludwig von Zinzendorf: Materialen und Dokumente. Erich Beyreuther and Gerhard Meyer, eds., 3rd ser., vol. 4, pp. 32–88. Reprint, Hildesheim: Georg Olms Verlag, 1973.

———. *Zinzendorf und die Mystik.* Berlin: Christlicher Zeitschriften-Verlag, 1950.

Walch, Johann George. *Theologosiches Bedencken von der Beschaffenheit der Herrnhutischen Secte, und wie sich ein Landes-Herr in Ansehung derselbigen zu verhalten habe. . . .* 1749. In Nikolaus Ludwig von Zinzendorf: Materialien und Dokumente. Erich Beyreuther and Gerhard Meyer, eds., 2nd ser., vol. 16. Reprint, Hildesheim: Georg Olms Verlagsbuchhandlung, 1982.

Walsh, John. "Religious Societies: Methodist and Evangelical, 1738–1800." In *Voluntary Religion.* W. J. Sheils and Diana Wood, eds. Studies in Church History, vol. 23, pp. 279–302. Oxford: Basil Blackwell for the Ecclesiastical History Society, 1986.

Ward, W. R. "'An Awakened Christianity'. The Austrian Protestants and Their Neighbours in the Eighteenth Century." *Journal of Ecclesiastical History* 40 (1989):53–73.

———. "Orthodoxy, Enlightenment and Religious Revival." In *Religion and Humanism.* Keith Robbin, ed. Studies in Church History, vol. 17, pp. 275–96. Oxford: Basil Blackwell for the Ecclesiastical History Society, 1981.

———. "Power and Piety: The Origins of Religious Revival in the Early Eighteenth Century." *Bulletin of the John Rylands University Library of Manchester* 63 (1980):231–52.

———. "The Relations of Enlightenment and Religious Revival in Central Europe and in the English-Speaking World." In *Reform and Reformation: England and the Continent, c.1500–c1750.* Derek Baker, ed. Studies in Church History, subsidia 2, pp. 281–305. Oxford: Basil Blackwell for the Ecclesiastical History Society, 1979.

———. *The Protestant Evangelical Awakening.* Cambridge: Cambridge University Press, 1992.

Watson, David Lowes. "The Origins and Significance of the Early Methodist Class Meeting." Ph.D. diss., Duke University, 1978.

Watts, Michael R. *The Dissenters: From the Reformation to the French Revolution.* Oxford: Clarendon Press, 1978.

Weinlich, John Rudolph. *The Moravian Diaspora: a Study of the Societies of the Moravian Church within the Protestant State Churches of Europe,* Nazarath, PA: Moravian Historical Society, 1959.

Wendland, Walter. "Die pietistische Bekehrung." *Zeitschrift für Kirchengeschichte* 38 (1923): 193–238.

Wesley, Charles. *The Journal of the Rev. Charles Wesley, M.A., Sometime Student of Christ Church Oxford.* Thomas Jackson, ed., 2 vols. 1849. Reprint, Grand Rapids, MI: Baker Book House, 1980.

Wesley, John, ed. *A Christian Library: Consisting of Extracts and Abridgements of the Choicest Pieces of Practical Divinity Which Have Been Published in the English Tongue.* 30 vols. London: J. Kershaw, 1827.

———. *Explanatory Notes upon the New Testament.* 2 vols., n.d. Reprint, Grand Rapids, MI: Baker Book House, 1983.

———. *The Journal of the Rev. John Wesley, A.M. Sometime Fellow of Lincoln College, Oxford.* Nehemiah Curnock, ed., 8 vols. London: Robert Culley, 1909–16.

———. *Journals and Diaries I, 1735–38.* W. Reginald Ward and Richard P. Heitzenrater, eds., vol. 18 of *The Works of John Wesley,* Richard P. Heitzenrater and Frank Baker, eds. Nashville, TN: Abingdon Press, 1988.

————. *Letters I, 1721–1739.* Frank Baker, ed., vol. 25 of *The Works of John Wesley,* Frank Baker, ed. Oxford: Clarendon Press, 1980.

————. *Letters II, 1740–1755.* Frank Baker, ed., vol. 26 of *The Works of John Wesley.* Frank Baker, ed. Oxford: Clarendon Press, 1982.

————. *The Letters of the Rev. John Wesley, A.M. Sometime Fellow of Lincoln College, Oxford.* John Telford, ed., 8 vols. London: Epworth Press, 1931.

————. *Minutes of the Methodist Conferences, from the First Held in London by the Late Rev. John Wesley A.M., in the Year 1744.* London: John Mason, 1862.

————. *The Works of John Wesley.* Thomas Jackson, ed., 14 vols., 3rd ed. 1872. Reprint, Grand Rapids, MI: Baker Book House, 1979.

Widmaier, Rita. "Alter und neuer Empirismus zur Erfahrungslehre von Locke und Thomasius." In *Christian Thomasius, 1655–1728: Interpretationen zu Werk und Wirkung mit einer Bibliographie der neueren Thomasius-Literatur.* Werner Schneiders, ed. Studien zum achtzehnten Jahrhundert, pp. 95–114. Hamburg: Felix Meiner Verlag, 1989.

Wollstadt, Hans-Joachim. *Geordnetes Dienen in der christlichen Gemeinde.* Arbeiten zur Pastortheologie, vol. 4. Göttingen: Vandenhoeck & Ruprecht, 1966.

Zinzendorf, Nikolaus Ludwig von, ed. *Büdingische Sammlung einiger in die Kirchen-Historie einschlagender sonderlich neuerer Schriften.* 1742–46. In Nikolaus Ludwig von Zinzendorf: Ergänzungsbände zu den Hauptschriften. Erich Beyreuther and Gerhard Meyer, eds., vols. 7–9. Reprint, Hildesheim: Georg Olms Verlag, 1965–66.

————. *Die gegenwärtige Gestalt des Kreuz-Reichs Jesu in seiner Unschuld....* 1745. In Nikolaus Ludwig von Zinzendorf: Ergänzungsbände zu den Hauptschriften. Erich Beyreuther and Gerhard Meyer, eds., vols. 5. Reprint, Hildesheim: Georg Olms Verlag, 1965.

————. *Des Ordinarii Fratrum berlinische Reden.* 1758. In Nikolaus Ludwig von Zinzendorf: Hauptschriften. Erich Beyreuther and Gerhard Meyer, eds., vol. 1. Reprint, Hildesheim: Georg Olms Verlag, 1962.

————. *Sieben letzte Reden so er in der Gemeine vor seiner am 7. Aug. erfolgten abermahligen Abreise nach America, gehalten.* 1743. In Nikolaus Ludwig von Zinzendorf: Hauptschriften. Erich Beyreuther and Gerhard Meyer, eds., vol. 2. Reprint, Hildesheim: Georg Olms Verlag, 1963.

————. *Sonderbare Gespräche zwischen einem Reisenden und allerhand andern Personen, von allerley in der Religion vorkommenden Wahrheiten.* 1739. In Nikolaus Ludwig von Zinzendorf: Hauptschriften. Beyreuther and Gerhard Meyer, eds., vol. 1. Reprint, Hildesheim: Georg Olms Verlag, 1962.

————. *Der teutsche Sokrates, das ist: Aufrichtige Anzeige verschiedener nicht so wohl unbkannter als vielmehr in Abfall gerathener Haupt-Wahrheiten in den Jahren 1725 und 1726.* 1732. Inn Nikolaus Ludwig von Zinzendorf: Hauptschriften. Erich Beyreuther and Gerhard Meyer, eds., vol. 1. Reprint, Hildesheim: Georg Olms Verlag, 1962.

Index